The Four Colors of
Business Growth

The Four Colors of Business Growth

Anjan V. Thakor

Washington University
St. Louis, Missouni

AMSTERDAM • BOSTON • HEIDELBERG • LONDON • NEW YORK • OXFORD
PARIS • SAN DIEGO • SAN FRANCISCO • SINGAPORE • SYDNEY • TOKYO
Academic Press is an imprint of Elsevier

Academic Press is an imprint of Elsevier
525 B Street, Suite 1800, San Diego CA 92101, USA
The Boulevard, Langford Lane, Kidlington, Oxford, OX5 1GB, UK

Notices
Knowledge and best practice in this field are constantly changing. As new
research and experience broaden our understanding, changes in research methods,
professional practices, or medical treatment may become necessary.

Practitioners and researchers must always rely on their own experience and
knowledge in evaluating and using any information, methods, compounds, or
experiments described herein. In using such information or methods they
should be mindful of their own safety and the safety of others, including
parties for whom they have a professional responsibility.

To the fullest extent of the law, neither the publisher nor the authors, contributors,
or editors, assume any liability for any injury and/or damage to persons or
property as a matter of products liability, negligence or otherwise, or from any
use or operation of any methods, products, instructions, or ideas contained
in the material herein.

Library of Congress Cataloging-in-Publication Data
Thakor, Anjan V.
 The four colors of business growth / Anjan V. Thakor.
    p. cm.
  ISBN 978-0-12-385239-7
 1. Corporations–Growth. 2. Strategic planning. 3. Business planning.
I. Title.
  HD2746.T52 2011
  658.4'06—dc23   2011019247

British Library Cataloguing-in-Publication Data
A catalogue record for this book is available from the British Library

For information on all Academic Press publications visit our
website at www.elsevierdirect.com

Printed and bound by CPI Group (UK) Ltd, Croydon, CR0 4YY

Transferred to digital print 2013

Working together to grow
libraries in developing countries

www.elsevier.com | www.bookaid.org | www.sabre.org

ELSEVIER   BOOK AID International   Sabre Foundation

This book is dedicated to the loving memory of my parents Lata and Viru, who taught me so much that the debt can never be repaid, to my wife Serry and our sons Richard and Cullen, who have both grown up to be fine young men and have taught me much. Their love and support have helped me to grow.

Contents

PREFACE xi

ABOUT THE AUTHOR xiii

CHAPTER 1   Growth Is Everywhere 1
   Lessons 8
      Reflection Exercise.. 10

CHAPTER 2   Growth Comes in Four Colors 13
   The Competing Values Framework for Growth..................... 19
   The CVF, Leadership, and Organizational Alignment 24
   Lessons 25
      Reflection Exercise.. 27

CHAPTER 3   The Competing Values Framework Growth
      Strategies and the Stock Market................................ 29
   Designing the Empirical Tests 31
   Lessons 37
      Reflection Exercise.. 38

CHAPTER 4   How to Know Which Color Your Growth
      Strategy Should Be.. 41
   The Seven-Step Strategy Formulation Process 42
      Step 1: Understand "What's a Growth Strategy?" 42
      Step 2: Define Value Driver—What It Is 43
      Step 3: Value Driver—Understand What It Is Not...................... 44
      Step 4: Develop a Shared Understanding of
         Core Competence 44
      Step 5: What Is a Core Competence?.. 44
      Step 6: Use Examples of Value Drivers and Strategies.............. 45
      Step 7: Develop a Simple Strategy Statement and
         Communicate, Communicate, and Communicate 47
      Two More Steps 49
   Lessons 51
      Reflection Exercise.. 51

CHAPTER 5   Alignment for Growth: The CVF's Power in Aligning
             Organizations through a Common Language 53
             The Power of a Common Language... 56
                 When the Power of a Common Language Is the Greatest 58
             Lessons.. 64
                 Reflection Exercise... 65

CHAPTER 6   Ideas for Yellow Growth Strategies 67
             How to Become a Better Yellow... 68
             Why Positive Factors Don't Get More Attention 70
             Beyond Abundance—Other Aspects of a
                 Yellow Culture and Growth Strategy 74
             What a Strong Yellow Culture Does for Organizations 75
             Tools for Developing Leaders 77
                 A Very Strong Corporate Culture.. 78
                 Organizations Develop Employees as Leaders 78
                 Commit to Employee Development 78
             Lessons.. 79
                 Reflection Exercise... 79

CHAPTER 7   Ideas for Red Growth Strategies 81
             What Good Red Companies Do To Grow................................ 83
             What Leaders Need To Understand About Execution 84
             What Is a Culture Focused on Execution?............................. 86
             Putting the Right People in the Right Place 88
             Performance Metrics and Alignment...................................... 90
                 Metrics Are Linked to Value Creation...................................... 90
                 Metrics Are Linked to the Growth Strategy 90
                 Performance Metrics Are Not Plentiful 91
             Lessons.. 91
                 Reflection Exercise... 92

CHAPTER 8   Ideas for Blue Growth Strategies 95
             Growth Strategies of Blue Companies.................................... 96
                 Mergers and Acquisitions 97
                 Divestitures 102
                 Establish a Market Niche and Develop a Brand...................... 106
                 Extend Products and Services to New Markets 108
                 Develop New Products and Services.. 110
             Respond to Market Changes in Your Value Driver 112
             Lessons.. 113
                 Reflection Exercise.. 114

CHAPTER 9   Ideas for Green Growth Strategies 117
             Green's Breakthough Ideas 120
                 What Is Innovation?...120
                 Why Is Innovation So Difficult?..121
             Does Innovation Have Any Generalizable Principles? 121
                 Principle 1: Combine and Hitchhike to Innovate 121

Principle 2: Diversity of Viewpoints Facilitates Innovation 124
Principle 3: Innovation Depends on How Many Shots
 You Take at the Basket 125
Principle 4: Set Up Your Reward–Punishment
 System to Punish Inaction, Not Failure and/or Defiance........125
Principle 5: Shelter Creative Work... 126
Principle 6: Create a Sense of Destiny and Don't Let
 the Creative Team Get Too Comfortable............................... 127
Principle 7: Remember the SPSS Rule of Innovation................ 128
Principle 8: Hire People You Don't Need................................... 129
Principle 9: Create Organizational Slack................................... 130
Principle 10: Innovation Pays Off, Often in Unpredictable
 Ways through Secondary Applications.................................. 131
Principle 11: All Innovation Challenges and Discards
 a Well-Accepted Assumption—Rule? Truth?......................... 133
Principle 12: Excessive Expertise Inhibits Innovation 135
The Process of Innovation... 136
Some Thoughts on Innovation Opportunities
 for the Future.. 137
  Solar Panels 137
  Gasoline Garden... 138
  Wind Power from the Stratosphere 138
  Ubiquitous Sensors 138
  Bacterial Toothpaste 139
Lessons 139
  Reflection Exercise... 140

CHAPTER 10 Wrapping Up... 141
Interpenetration of Opposites: Embracing the Paradox 142
Designing and Implementing a Growth Strategy................ 144
Concluding Message 145
  Reflection Exercise... 146

APPENDIX... 149

RESOURCES AND ADDITIONAL READINGS 157

INDEX.. 161

Preface

In the summer of 1996, I moved as a senior faculty member to The University of Michigan Business School, and over the better part of the next decade I worked closely with three very talented colleagues on issues of organization, change, culture, and growth. These colleagues were Kim Cameron, Bob Quinn, and Jeff DeGraff. Our work was with various companies in the context of leadership development programs. Over the course of that collaboration, we developed a robust and holistic framework, called the Competing Values Framework (CVF) for Growth, and I have used it ever since in work I have done with many organizations to help them reposition themselves for value-enhancing growth.

One of my dreams has been to write an easily accessible business book that would convey the essence of what my colleagues and I have learned over many years of research, teaching, and consulting on this issue. This book is the result.

The book has two main goals. First, it will show you how to gain clarity on your growth strategy. One key to this is figuring out an effective *communication strategy*. This book provides a framework for developing such a strategy and achieving *alignment* on your strategy both internally within the organization and externally with stakeholders such as financiers. Second, it will show you how to get the biggest bang for the buck from your focused strategy.

The imperative for growth is simple. It is as simple as "get busy growing or get busy dying." Growth excites. Growth regenerates. Without growth there is stagnation, which eventually leads to decay . . . and death. This is just as true for organizations as it is for individuals. This does *not* mean that it is always a good idea for every organization to seek to grow its top line at every point in time. Sometimes value can be created by shrinking rather than growing. But few disagree that, over the long haul, the pursuit of growth is one of their goals. How do you position the organization for explosive growth? That's what this book is about.

The first chapter sets up the main points of the book. It addresses the issue of *why* growth is important. It explains the crucial role played by *alignment* in the successful execution of a growth strategy and the importance of communication.

Chapter 2 introduces the CVF for Growth, and Chapter 3 summarizes the research results linking growth strategies to stock market valuation.

Chapter 4 develops the key ideas needed to uncover an explosive growth strategy and to discover *how* to communicate this strategy to external constituents and to the organization. Effective communication is the key to alignment. Chapter 5 shows how the CVF can help you deal with one of the biggest internal challenges every leader faces—*alignment*. This chapter is devoted to one of the main messages of the book.

The next four chapters—Chapters 6 through 9—deal with the specifics of growth strategies in each of the four quadrants of the CVF: Yellow (People), Red (Process), Blue (Competition), and Green (Innovation). In each chapter, there is a discussion of the specific approach to gaining alignment. While communication is the common element across all four quadrants, the approach to gaining alignment varies from one quadrant to the next. Chapter 10 wraps up.

Like its basic premise that growth is an imperative for renewal and survival, the main message of this book itself is simple: Once a growth strategy is identified, effective execution requires alignment. The basic ideas around alignment and growth are universal in their applicability. And they provide readily implementable road maps for organizational change.

The book has benefitted from comments from various people, most notably Sam Chun, Mark Fuerer, and Lee Konczak. My many thanks to them. I also thank Christine Hatina for her excellent assistance in typing this manuscript.

About the Author

Value-Enhancing Strategist

A foremost researcher and respected authority on issues regarding finance and banking, Anjan Thakor offers a deeply knowledgeable perspective on the subject of value creation. He has shared his wisdom with many Fortune 500 leaders including clients such as Anheuser-Busch, Association of Corporate Growth, Borg-Warner Automotive, Brown Shoe, Bunge, Citigroup, Farm Credit System, FBI, MECS, Nestle Purina, RGA, Thompson-Reuters, Waxman Industries, and Whirlpool. In addition to his work with U.S. companies, he has also interacted with and advised corporate executives all over the world—Europe, as well as the emerging markets in Brazil and China.

Scholarship

Dr. Thakor is Director of the PhD Program, Director of the Institute for Innovation and Growth and John E. Simon Professor of Finance at Olin Business School at Washington University in St. Louis, Missouri. He served on the faculties of The University of Michigan and Indiana University prior to Olin, winning teaching excellence awards at all three schools. He was also a visiting professor at UCLA and Northwestern University.

A partner of the Competing Values Company, a consulting firm that assists leaders in facilitating change, innovation, and growth, Dr. Thakor, additionally, is an advisor with the Innovatrium Institute for Innovation, an innovation lab in Ann Arbor, Michigan. He has received research grants through the Bank Administration Institute, Federal Home Loan Bank Board, Garn Institute of Finance, Prochnow Educational Foundation, and the U.S. Treasury Department.

As Director of the Institute for Innovation and Growth (IIG) at the Olin School of Business at Washington University, Dr. Thakor guides research on a variety of issues related to the emerging frontiers in creativity, innovation, and organizational growth. The IIG produces books and white papers on innovation and engages in research and other types of corporate intervention projects with companies to help reinvigorate their growth engines.

He has made significant contributions to his field. Dr. Thakor is former Managing Editor of the *Journal of Financial Intermediation* and past president of the Financial Intermediation Research Society. He has published more than 100 articles and seven books. His research has been published in leading economics and finance journals, among them *American Economic Review, The Review of Economic Studies, The RAND Journal of Economics, The Economic Journal, The Journal of Finance, The Journal of Economic Theory, The Journal of Financial Economics, The Journal of Financial Intermediation,* and *The Review of Financial Studies.* His books include *Handbook of Financial Intermediation and Banking; Competing Values Leadership; Contemporary Financial Intermediation; The Value Sphere; Becoming a Better Value Creator; Designing Financial Systems in Transition Economies;* and *Credit, Intermediation, and the Macro Economy.* He holds a PhD in finance from the Kellogg School at Northwestern University.

In an article published in 2008, he was identified as the fourth most prolific researcher in the world in finance over the past 50 years based on publications in the top seven finance journals during that time. In addition to his publications, Dr. Thakor has been actively involved in advising PhD students who have gone on to enjoy distinguished academic careers. He has chaired the dissertation committees of 30 students who have received their PhDs, and two of his former students are now his colleagues at Washington University in St. Louis. He has won numerous teaching awards in the MBA, Executive MBA, and PhD programs.

Corporate Consulting and Expert Witness Work

Dr. Thakor is actively involved in corporate consultancy and expert witness work, including extensive work in corporate finance and banking.

He is a frequent speaker at corporate events and has helped various types of organizations, including numerous Fortune 500 firms, navigate the complexities of financing, capital investment, and performance evaluation for strategic decision making. Present and past clients include Citigroup, Reuters, CIGNA, Whirlpool, Dana, RR Donnelley, Anheuser-Busch, The Limited, Landscape Structures, Allison Engine, Borg-Warner Automotive, Enterprise Car Rental, Spartech, Smurfit Stone, Nestle-Purina, Bunge, Brown Shoe, The Farm Credit System, and Essex Corporation.

He has worked extensively with boards of directors of various organizations. His clients have included public and private firms, as well as small, medium, and large ones in a variety of industries. In addition, he has served as an expert witness in cases involving banking and finance issues and testified in federal courts on various occasions.

CHAPTER 1

Growth Is Everywhere

> Where this is no vision, people perish.
> – Proverbs 29:18

Who were the ten richest people at the end of 2007? According to *Forbes*, "The World's Billionaires," March 5, 2008, they were: Warren Buffet, Carlos Slim Helu and family, William Gates III, Lakshmi Mittal, Mukesh Ambani, Anil Ambani, Ingvar Kamprad and family, K.P. Singh, Oleg Deripaska, and Karl Albrecht. An interesting list, but not one that most people would have predicted a decade ago!

Warren Buffet   Carlos Slim Helu

William Gates III   Lakshmi Mittal   Mukesh Ambani

Anil Ambani   Ingvar Kamprad

K.P. Singh   Oleg Deripaska   Karl Albrecht

Perhaps just as interestingly, this list had changed by 2009, so that Mukesh Ambani, an Indian industrialist, had overtaken Bill Gates as the richest person in the world. Write down the three most interesting observations that occur to you as you look at the photos.

_____

_____

_____

Here are a few observations about what is most interesting:

- The large number of rich people from the so-called "developing" nations. This number is expected to grow in the future as it is predicted that 86% of the world's population will be residing in the emerging markets by the year 2050.

- The number of people who have become rich with entrepreneurial activities in industries that were viewed as "commoditized" (read "dogs"!) just a few years ago.

- What has made these people so rich is growth.

If there is one theme that stands out worldwide in the past decade, it's growth. Growth is all around us. Everywhere. In 2007, the average annual GDP growth rates for different countries in the world were: United States, 2.0%[1]; countries in the European Union, 3%; India, 9.6%; China, 11.9%; Brazil, 5.7%; Liberia, 9.4%; and the Sudan, 10.2%.

The figures for sub-Saharan Africa are particularly interesting because it is a region that for many years had not participated in global economic growth. While the global recession that began in 2008 has dampened the momentum created by this economic growth, leading to a contraction of the global economy in 2008–2009, we should not forget the impressive global economic advances of the last decade.

---

[1] The average GDP growth rate for the U.S. economy was 2.7% during 2000–2007. Had it not been for the significant weakening of the dollar during this time period, the average annual growth rate in GDP would have been 3.7% for the U.S. See John Heim, "How Falling Exchange Rates 2000–2007 Have Affected the U.S. Economy and Trade Deficit," Rensselaer Working Papers in Economics #0801, January 2008.

Two facts are striking about this global economic growth. First, it has come during a period of substantial political and military instability in the world. Second, quite a bit of this growth was achieved by industries that had previously been somewhat disparagingly classified as "commodity businesses." Specifically, businesses in industries where money is made on volume, not margins. And since the margins are thin because of competitive pressures, there's not a lot of money to be made. Yet, what did we see?

The Mittals from India, now based in London, bought up steel mills dirt-cheap all over the world and built the world's leading steel conglomerate. Another Indian firm, Tata, has introduced the first $2500 automobile in the world. And with Tata's purchase of Land Rover and Jaguar from Ford, the company has access to a global auto dealership network to boot.

All this in an industry in which the product is considered so commoditized that so many car manufacturers are in a constant struggle for survival, and GM and Chrysler have needed emergency loans from the government just to stay afloat.

What made all this possible? Many factors came together to make it happen. Perhaps the most important was the fact that countries with huge pools of human talent but widespread intervention by government bureaucracies in their economies decided to lift some of their self-imposed shackles.

As Brazil, China, and India opened up segments of their economies, they created the conditions for foreign investment capital to flow in, and this stimulated economic growth. But even more important, it created fertile ground in which domestic entrepreneurs could plant their new ideas and flourish.

Many of these entrepreneurs operated "outside the box." Perhaps because there was *no* box to start with in which they *could* operate! Preconceived notions about what's a growth business and what's not were jettisoned. So too were ideas about what is possible and what is not. Why not a $2500 car?

What's next—a below-$100 washing machine, a truly enjoyable flying experience in coach on a commercial airline, quantum computing, computers that operate in response to hand gestures without a keyboard, the ability of an individual to become physically invisible, a world where no human being goes hungry? Look around you. It's all either here or on the horizon!

The other force that shaped these events is the enormous growth in highly educated young people in many countries, especially the emerging-market countries. China and India turn out millions of university-trained engineers every year. That's what allows a company like IBM to set up shop in India with 80,000 employees and have most of its code writing done there.

The large number of educated people in foreign countries is what allows a company like Emerson Electric to shift some product development to China, where the plentiful supply of talented engineers permits "swarm engineering"—committing a large number of engineers to a specific project—and more rapid product development. It is what permits U.S. companies to outsource back-office functions to India and the Philippines. The net result? Lower costs, higher-quality products and services, and enormous benefits for everyone.

But all of this global growth has also created numerous tensions. As the developing countries have experienced rapid growth, they have increased their demand for natural resources. Oil, steel, food, and other natural resources are now in higher demand because they are needed to satisfy the ravenous appetites for them in the rapidly growing emerging economies. This has not only increased the prices of these commodities worldwide, but also has led to heightened price volatility. And the accompanying redistribution of wealth to resource-rich countries has generated political tensions.

Let us now take this notion of growth to organizations. What do we mean by "growth" for an organization? It can be many things. For example, it can mean getting bigger in terms of sales or assets. It can also mean doing and/or making new things without changing firm size. Or it can mean leaving old things behind for a while and repositioning for subsequent growth. It means *all* of these things.

There is only one alternative to growth. It is stagnation. So, in the long run, if you are not growing, you will wither away. Growth energizes. Growth liberates. Growth creates opportunities. These things are just as true for individuals and organizations as they are for countries. Of course, as a leader or shareholder in a publicly traded company, an important concern for you is shareholder value.

This raises the issue of how growth affects stock prices and stock returns. What does the stock market really value? Let's look at some more data, given in Figure 1.1.

The second row below the bar chart in this diagram indicates that all companies in the S&P 500 grew revenue every year on average. The first row says that the top 25% of companies in terms of average 10-year returns to shareholders delivered 25% shareholder returns (dividends plus price appreciation) *per year* for ten years. That's pretty impressive!

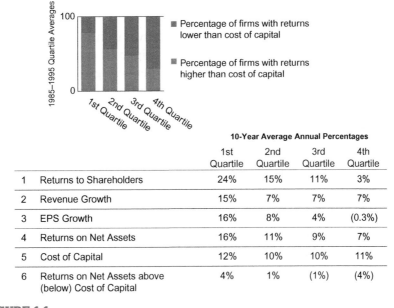

Standard & Poor's 500 Performance Quarterlies

- Percentage of firms with returns lower than cost of capital
- Percentage of firms with returns higher than cost of capital

10-Year Average Annual Percentages

		1st Quartile	2nd Quartile	3rd Quartile	4th Quartile
1	Returns to Shareholders	24%	15%	11%	3%
2	Revenue Growth	15%	7%	7%	7%
3	EPS Growth	16%	8%	4%	(0.3%)
4	Returns on Net Assets	16%	11%	9%	7%
5	Cost of Capital	12%	10%	10%	11%
6	Returns on Net Assets above (below) Cost of Capital	4%	1%	(1%)	(4%)

FIGURE 1.1

What does the stock market value?

The next 25% of companies delivered 15% shareholder returns per year. Not bad at all! Note that the companies that delivered higher shareholder returns also experienced higher revenue growth. So this is Lesson #1—the stock market demands growth.

Lesson #2 can be gleaned by observing that the companies in the top two quartiles of shareholder returns delivered higher returns to their shareholders than the cost of the capital given to them by their shareholders. That is what we call "good growth."

The bottom two quartiles don't do as well. The third quartile delivered 11% shareholder returns per year, 1% below the cost of capital. The fourth quartile delivered 3% shareholder returns per year, a whopping 4% below the cost of capital.

The bottom two quartiles of companies did grow their revenues. But their growth is what we call "bad growth." Because these companies delivered returns to their shareholders that fell below the cost of capital, they destroyed value.

Let's focus on the companies that delivered good growth. We can see from the diagram that these companies did two things better than others. First, they grew revenues at a healthy clip, and earnings per share even more impressively. In fact, the 16% per-year growth in earnings per share is downright giddy! Even Warren Buffett advises CEOs not to promise an earnings-per-share growth exceeding 15% because it is so difficult to achieve. Second, they created value for their shareholders as they grew.

Good growth is not easy. There are typically far more examples of companies that achieved growth than there are of companies that achieved *good* growth. An example of good growth is that achieved by Arena Resources, Inc., which grew its sales revenue 158.3% during 2007 and also quadrupled its stock price during that time.

By contrast, Home Depot grew its sales from $55.5 billion in 2001 to $77.3 billion by end 2007, but its stock price went from $45.53 at the end of 2001 to $25.73 at the end of 2007, both stock prices adjusted for dividends. That is growth, but not good growth.

Why is good growth so difficult? Because it paradoxically requires the organization to move in two opposite directions at the same time. High growth requires change. High growth requires accepting risk. Delivering shareholder returns above the cost of capital requires stability within the firm. It requires discipline. It calls for avoiding gambles that don't have a high likelihood of paying off.

These disciplined approaches are not always compatible with high growth. Difficult or not, good growth has its rewards for the company. This is not only in terms of happy shareholders, but also in terms of employee pride and positive energy.

Another reason why good growth is hard is that achieving it consistently requires *organizational alignment.* By this I mean that there is internal alignment—employees as well as the Board of Directors understand and agree with the mission, vision, and growth strategy of the organization and are committed to making the strategy a success. Such alignment is critical for employee *motivation.*

By organizational alignment I also mean that there is *external alignment*—shareholders, creditors, and other key stakeholders also understand and agree with the mission, vision, and growth strategy of the organization. Research has shown, however, that disagreement is commonplace and achieving alignment in the face of disagreement remains one of the major challenges, as well as an important goal, for organizational leaders.[2]

What are the secrets of good growth? How did Starbucks and Apple do it? What about Dell? How did IBM achieve good growth? What's common? What's different? How did they achieve alignment? This is what we turn to in the next chapter.

---

[2] See Amy Dittmar and Anjan V. Thakor, "Why Do Firms Issue Equity?" *Journal of Finance* 62 (1), 2007, pp. 1–54; Anjan Thakor, "Managerial Decisions, Control Influences and Corporate Finance: Survey Evidence," Working Paper, Washington University in St. Louis, 2009; and Eric Van den Steen, "Impersonal Authority in a Theory of the Firm," *American Economic Review*, forthcoming.

LESSONS

If you are a senior executive in an organization, what can you take away from all this?

- The key lesson is that the stock market rewards *good* growth. It is not enough to just deliver good operating performance and profits. The market needs to see prospects for growth as well. There are scores of companies that managed their assets with great care and delivered good returns on assets, but did not grow much. Many of these companies ended up being targets for acquisitions as others saw opportunities for growth that these companies themselves did not.

  But growth has to enhance shareholder value—it has to be good growth. There are scores of companies that grew, but at rates of return on assets that fell short of the cost of capital, which destroyed value. They too became attractive acquisition targets or were subsequently forced to shrink or go out of business.

- Recognize that there is no such thing as a commodity business when it comes to growth. *Every* business can be a growth business. *Growth is a mindset.*

- Invest in developing the human capital in your workforce through continuing education. Growth often springs from unexpected sources. It is not always planned by your strategic planning staff. The more people you have who have the tools and knowledge to visualize possible opportunities for growth, the more ideas you will have to consider for adoption.

- The fact that Brazil, China, and India are developing more rapidly than many other nations is not an accident. Among other things, they have the largest pools of educated young people. Education develops not only talent but also the motivation and determination of your people. As former football coach Lou Holtz says in his book, *Winning Every Day*:

  Your talent determines what you can do. Your motivation determines how much you are willing to do. Your attitude determines how well you do it.

- Remove the obstacles to growth that are embedded in your organization—just the way the governments in India and China have begun to remove the impediments to entrepreneurial growth that for so long gripped their economies. We will spend quite a lot of time discussing how you can discover where these obstacles lie in your organization and what to do about them. A major obstacle is often lack of *internal* and *external alignment.* We will see some tools that can be used to improve alignment.

- Understand that growth rarely comes without organizational tensions. Just as global growth has created its own tensions, so will the growth in your organization. Do you know what they are? These tensions impede alignment, so it is important to know how to anticipate, diagnose, and cope with them. These are topics for later chapters.

As you read the rest of this book, keep the following in mind. Despite the economic funk created by the recession of 2008–2009, the imperative for value creation is still growth. The winners of the new decade are looking beyond mere survival. They are planning their growth strategies for the future. If your plans do not involve growth, you're either too big or you're leaving money on the table!

Reflection Exercise

As a leader in your organization, please choose a number from 1 to 5 to assign to each statement in Exercise 1.1.

Exercise 1.1

1 = Strongly disagree; 2 = Disagree; 3 = Neither agree nor disagree; 4 = Agree; 5 = Strongly agree

	1	2	3	4	5
(i) While our business operates in an intensely competitive industry, we have never viewed our product/service as (almost) a commodity on which healthy margins cannot be earned.			/		
(ii) Our organization widely shares the belief that growing sales revenue at 5% or more per year in the foreseeable future is a reasonable target.	/				
(iii) Our key people have the skills, imagination, and conviction that will permit us to aggressively pursue our target of 5% or more sales revenue growth per year.				/	
(iv) We have a clear understanding of the organizational tensions our future growth will create.		/			
(v) We believe we can achieve our growth targets with good growth.			/		
(vi) Over the past 10 years, our average annual sales revenue growth rate has exceeded that of all our peers.			/		
(vii) Over the past 10 years, our earnings per share growth rate has exceeded that of all our peers.			/		
(viii) Over the past 10 years, our return on net assets has exceeded our cost of capital every year and our spread has exceeded that of all our peers.			/		
(ix) Our organization would not undertake initiatives to grow sales unless these would be expected to generate returns on net assets exceeding our cost of capital.			/		

not involved in these elements

- What overall score did you come up with? (*Hint:* Any score below 4 leaves considerable room for improvement.)

- What did you learn?

- Contact the top executives in your organization and ask them to provide their scores.

- Meet and discuss these scores. What is the degree of alignment among the top executives on the issues?

- What ideas have different executives come up with as a result of this exercise?

- What are the concrete action steps that can be taken in response to these executives' ideas?

CHAPTER 2

Growth Comes in Four Colors

> Man is not the sum of what he has but the totality of
> what he does not yet have, of what he might have.
> — Jean-Paul Sartre

Under CEO Richard Mahoney, Monsanto transformed itself from an industrial chemicals firm into a knowledge-driven life-sciences firm that focuses on biotechnology. Chemicals were viewed as a commodity and thus these businesses were divested. This repositioning eventually led to good growth for the company. By contrast, Asahi Kasei, a Japanese firm focused on building a portfolio of diversified chemical products, has created a growth machine in chemical manufacturing.

Positioning its more mature and domestic-focused businesses as a stable source of earnings, Asahi Kasei has been investing aggressively in high-growth global sectors such as specialty chemicals, electronic materials, and devices. Shiro Hiruta, president and CEO, said:

> Our strategy of focusing on value-added products with high profitability
> has proved its worth. Despite the rise in the price of oil, we've managed
> to achieve our revenue targets ahead of schedule.[1]

McDonald's has become one of the most well-recognized brand names in the world by adopting a growth strategy based on franchising most of its stores. The economic rationale was simple. Franchising

---

[1] See *Fortune*, July 21, 2008.

reduces McDonald's own capital investment. And it also generates better incentives, as the franchisee is an owner of the store rather than an employee of McDonald's.

By contrast, Starbucks has achieved spectacular growth with a strategy that calls for the company to own most of its stores. And counter to what most management strategy gurus prescribe, it is also vertically integrated.

The point is this: Companies achieve growth with a dizzying variety of growth strategies. For every company that adopts one strategy successfully, you can find another that achieves as much success with an opposite strategy. This makes it difficult to generalize based on anecdotes.

Perhaps this is just a reflection of the fact that the world is a complex place. But seeing the world as a complex mosaic of endless variety is not terribly helpful in making sense of it. What one needs is a way to organize this endless variety into a small number of categories and understand how these categories are related. Sort of like the way we think of food. There are hundreds of dishes in Italian cuisine and a similar amount of variety in the foods from many other countries.

The total number of distinct dishes from all over the world is so large that it would be virtually impossible to remember or make sense of the variety. But it helps enormously to think of food organized by country of origin, perhaps further categorizing it by the region of the country—like Chinese food categorized as Cantonese, Schezwan, and so on, or Italian food categorized as Northern and Southern Italian.

What we explore in this chapter is a framework that organizes growth strategies into just *four* categories. As we will see shortly, the framework is much more than a way to transform seemingly endless complexity into a parsimonious set of categories. It also helps leaders achieve organizational alignment for a chosen growth strategy.

To see this, let's consider some companies that have experienced stellar growth and see what they share. What do McKinsey, Ericsson, Wal-Mart, and Dell have in common when it comes to their growth strategies?

At one level, the answer seems to be: nothing. After all, these are very different companies. McKinsey is in management consulting. Ericsson is in telecommunications equipment and related services to mobile and fixed-network operations. Wal-Mart is a giant retailer. And Dell is a logistics specialist that sells personal computers.

But let's reflect on this a little. A significant part of McKinsey's success in achieving good growth is the strength of its internal community. This includes high performance through shared values, and inclusion, teamwork, and consensus. This approach of focusing on the organization's internal capability and culture helps to retain key employees and build effective relationships with customers. The result is improved customer service and good growth.

Similarly, Ericsson attempts to develop a high-performance culture by cultivating the generation of knowledge assets within the firm. Performance is enhanced through the development of new competencies, both at the organization and at the individual level. The result is greater information sharing, collaborative learning, and the emergence of effective new technologies that enhance Ericsson's growth prospects.

Wal-Mart is a retailing powerhouse. Most people know that one of the keys to Wal-Mart's success has been its pioneering inventory management processes, which have helped it to achieve outstanding inventory turnover and optimize asset utilization on the balance sheet. Its commitment to these processes has elevated its inventory management to a level that is the envy of most organizations.

The impact of this is that Wal-Mart has incurred a lower cost of carrying assets on its balance sheet. This cost saving has, in part, been passed along to the customer. Net result: lower prices for consumers and higher growth for Wal-Mart.

Dell, which transformed itself from a no-name PC maker into a power-house brand, has also prospered with a focus on its own processes. It is well-known for its excellence in efficiently knitting together a far-flung supply chain so tightly that many refer to it as more of a logistics company than a PC maker. Dell, however, has elevated itself far above its sell-direct business model. At the heart of its success is a penny-pinching, cost-conscious culture that constantly challenges the status quo.

Dell's focus on improving the efficiency of its internal processes is relentless. The result: an obsession with cutting costs and improving efficiency that leads to more competitive products in the marketplace. And leads to growth. However, the key value driver for Dell has shifted somewhat as consumers have become increasingly interested in product styling and being able to touch and feel products before purchase, leading to growth stagnation for the company in the past few years.

In fact, one could argue that part of Dell's problem is that it has been *too* cost-focused. The resulting lack of innovation has made it challenging for Dell to deal with a shift in its value driver.[2]

It should be apparent by now that what McKinsey and Ericsson have in common is a focus on their human capital within the firm. Top-line growth is fueled by investing in this human capital, and strengthening the organization culture that wraps around this human capital. Each organization is aligned behind this focus.

What Wal-Mart and Dell have in common is a focus on their internal processes that drive constant improvements in efficiency. Top-line growth is stoked by process enhancements that cut costs and improve the quality of products, services, and customer-interface processes. Again, each organization has a culture that reflects strong alignment on the pivotal importance of internal processes and efficiency.

What all four companies share is that they look *inward* first as a way to increase their external competitiveness and achieve top-line growth

---

[2] As most people know, Dell has struggled mightily as stiff competition and the sagging global economy have taken their toll, driving Dell's stock price down from more than $30 in late 2007 to under $10 per share in 2009. By 2011, it had rebounded to around $15, but shareholder returns have not been impressive.

targets. The inward focus of McKinsey and Ericsson is on the people and the organization. The inward focus of Wal-Mart and Dell is on the processes that drive various behaviors in the organization.

This is not to suggest that McKinsey and Ericsson don't have good processes, or that Wal-Mart and Dell don't focus on their people. Of course they do. Rather, what is being suggested here is that there are specific dimensions in which each of these companies has chosen a path that puts it in a class of its own in that dimension. While these organizations do many things very well, each also exhibits a unique talent in one dimension that few others can match.

Moving on, what do Coca-Cola, Berkshire Hathaway, Google, and Apple have in common? Going beyond the obvious computing technology focus in two out of these four firms, the answer is that they are all masters at interacting with their external constituents: shareholders, customers, and suppliers. Each company has created enormous amounts of shareholder value by doing so.

But among these four, Coca-Cola and Berkshire Hathaway fall into one group, and Google and Apple fall into another. Consider Coca-Cola and Berkshire Hathaway as a group. Both have excelled in gaining market share, responding quickly to new opportunities in the market as they presented themselves, delivering excellent short-term results, dominating through acquisitions and alliances, and effectively utilizing their analytical skills and customer knowledge to achieve top-line growth.

Coca-Cola was the first major company to adopt Economic Value Added (EVA) to assess the financial performance of its business units in a more holistic way than traditional accounting measures of performance permit. It was also aggressive in recognizing the enormous market potential of bottled water and gaining a foothold in that market with Dasani.

Berkshire Hathaway, with Warren Buffett at the helm, has been in the top quartile of firms in terms of delivering shareholder returns for over four decades. It has used prudent financial management and acquisitions as a way to sustain impressive growth. For example, witness the way the company stepped up the growth rate at Geico, an insurance company it acquired a few years ago, and made it a household name in insurance.

By contrast, Google and Apple have prospered by focusing on innovation. Their approach to growth has been through product innovation, disruptive change that redefines entire industries, risk seeking, and the pursuit of uniqueness. Google created a whole new industry through its search engine technology. And today Google is a dominant brand name worldwide.

Apple, on the brink of bankruptcy in 1997, brought cofounder Steve Jobs back to lead the company, and he transformed it with a whoosh. Apple's foray into consumer retailing not only set the company on a new path of innovation and growth, but also introduced disruptive change in the music industry.

We see then that while Coca-Cola, Berkshire Hathaway, Google, and Apple all have in common the ability to interact effectively with external constituencies, they also differ in important ways. Coca-Cola and Berkshire Hathaway are focused more on the here and now, on the markets and opportunities that exist *today*.

By contrast, Google and Apple chose growth strategies that were more focused on creating *new* markets—more on new opportunities and things that were unprecedented. Before Google, no firm provided the kind of at-your-fingertips search capability that we now take for granted. Before Apple, no firm had provided the combination of PC technology and access to music that is now so ubiquitous.

THE COMPETING VALUES FRAMEWORK FOR GROWTH

Our discussion thus far has illustrated four categories of growth. (See Figure 2.1.) One way to think about this framework is that it helps reduce to four the number of growth strategies firms employ, so we can better see the connections and the patterns in the data.

Firms that gain a competitive advantage in growth through a focus on their own people and organization culture, like McKinsey and

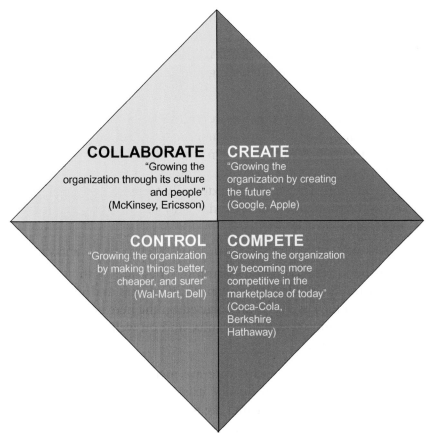

COLLABORATE
"Growing the organization through its culture and people"
(McKinsey, Ericsson)

CREATE
"Growing the organization by creating the future"
(Google, Apple)

CONTROL
"Growing the organization by making things better, cheaper, and surer"
(Wal-Mart, Dell)

COMPETE
"Growing the organization by becoming more competitive in the marketplace of today"
(Coca-Cola, Berkshire Hathaway)

FIGURE 2.1
Competing Values Framework for growth.

Ericsson, fall into the COLLABORATE quadrant. Firms that drive growth through enhanced internal processes and efficiency, such as Wal-Mart and Dell, fall in the CONTROL quadrant.

Firms with a growth agenda that is fueled by more effective interactions with external stakeholders and dominating the markets that exist today, like Coca-Cola and Berkshire Hathaway, fall in the COMPETE quadrant. And firms that predicate their growth strategies on innovation and disruptive change, like Google and Apple, fall in the CREATE quadrant.

The colors are important because they become a handy source of reference to various forms of value creation and also make it easy for people to remember the categories. COLLABORATE is Yellow, CONTROL is Red, COMPETE is Blue, and CREATE is Green.[3] While this taxonomy is useful, there is a more interesting and powerful message hidden in this framework.

To see this, let us slice the picture vertically. Now we can see that Collaborate and Control share something in common. They are both internally focused—Collaborate on the organization's people and Control on its processes. Likewise, Compete and Create share something in common. They are both externally focused—Compete on the markets and customers that exist today, and Create on the markets and customers of tomorrow.

Now slice the picture horizontally. We can see that Control and Compete have something in common. They are both focused on short-term results, replicating past rules of success and improving on things done in the past. Both are focused on the here and now, on tangible outcomes and measurable results, and on well-defined timelines for achieving results.

By contrast, Collaborate and Create are focused on creating capabilities and opportunities that do not exist today—on things that have unpredictable timelines for achieving results and on outcomes that are often ambiguous and difficult to measure.

---

[3]The association of a particular color with a specific quadrant is arbitrary. We could have chosen any color for any quadrant.

So, as we move from the left to the right in the picture, the focus of growth strategy shifts from developing and utilizing internal capability to harvesting external opportunity. As one moves from the bottom to the top, the focus of growth strategy shifts from short time horizons and control over outcomes to longer, less predictable time horizons and a willingness to be flexible. (See Figure 2.2.)

We can see now that no matter which way we slice the model, the diagonally opposite quadrants have *nothing* in common. In fact, it's more dramatic than that. The growth perspective that drives Control is the *opposite* of the one that drives Create. Control focuses on growth through efficiency, cost reduction, and predictability of outcomes. It seeks stability. Create, by contrast, thrives on chaos and lack of predictability. It seeks to disrupt rather than stabilize!

A similar contrast holds true for Collaborate and Compete. Firms in Collaborate seek to foster internal stability, security, and growth in the face of uncertainty. They assume that the external environment is best

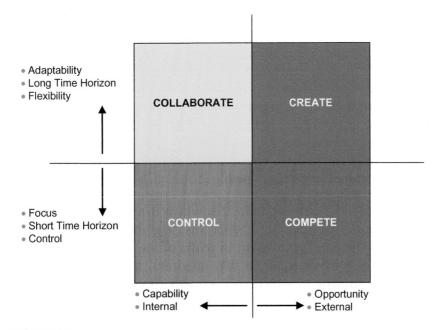

FIGURE 2.2
The progression of the Competing Values Framework.

managed through commitment and cooperation. They view customers as partners in an extended community. Loyalty flows up, down, and across such organizations.

By contrast, firms in Compete perceive the external world as hostile and customers as self-interested and choosy. They judge their success on market share, revenue, brand equity, profitability, and shareholder value.

The diagonally opposite quadrants thus focus on *competing* forms of growth. *At the margin*, a move in one direction inevitably implies an immediate move *away* from the diagonally opposite direction. This is why it is called the *Competing Values Framework* (CVF).

So what does that mean? Two things. First, an organization must choose the primary quadrant of its growth strategy. Those that try to do everything achieve nothing. A certain degree of focus is essential. And focus implies choice. This is particularly compelling because these different growth strategies tug against each other and pull the organization in different directions.

Second, to the extent that an organization's growth strategy spans multiple quadrants, it is crucial for its leaders to recognize the inherent *tensions* that such a strategy generates. An organization that attempts to grow with a Compete growth strategy will not find it easy to build a collaborative workplace with large investments in employee development and satisfaction. An organization focused on efficiency will not find it easy to foster an environment in which employees generate breakthrough new ideas for growth.

This can be seen clearly in Figure 2.3, which describes the characteristics of the different quadrants. What this diagram in the figure shows is that each quadrant is different in terms of the kinds of people who excel with growth strategies in that quadrant, the kind of organizational environment in which such growth strategies are successfully executed, and the performance metrics by which success is measured.

To see the most obvious contrasts, note that investing in training per employee (Collaborate) will, in the period in which the investment

COLLABORATE

People: Build trust, helpful, resolve conflicts, empowering, good listeners, encourage participation

Environment: Harmonious atmosphere, collaborative workplace, informal communication, shared values

Performance Metrics: Employee satisfaction,employee turnover, training per employee, competency, peer review

CREATE

People: Visionary, optimistic, generalist, enthusiastic, quick thinker, expressive

Environment: Stimulating projects, flexible hours, free from everyday constraints, diverse workforce

Performance Metrics: Diversity of experiments, new market growth, adoption rate, revenues from new products and services

CONTROL

People: Organized, methodical, technical, practical, objective, persistent

Environment: Clear roles, logical objectives, structured work, cohesive work processes

Performance Metrics: Budget adherence, milestones achieved, number of failures, regulatory compliance

COMPETE

People: Goal oriented, assertive, driven, accountable, decisive, competitive

Environment: High pressure, fast moving, quantifiable results, pay for performance

Performance Metrics: Gross profit, time to market, return on investment, operating income

FIGURE 2.3
What the CVF growth strategy genome looks like at the organization level.

is made, cause operating income and return on capital investment (Compete) to decline. Trying a diversity of experiments (Create) will typically come at the expense of minimizing the number of failures (Control). Thus, each choice has a cost. Indeed, if one goes too far in any quadrant, one ends up in the "negative zone" of that quadrant.

Each quadrant brings with it a virtue—a positive contribution to growth and value creation, which we shall refer to as the "positive zone" of the quadrant. The positive zone of Collaborate includes employee retention, harmony, and morale. The positive zone of Control includes efficiency, coordination, and predictability. The positive zone of Compete includes greater competitiveness, customer satisfaction, and shareholder value. The positive zone of Create includes innovation and high future growth potential.

But, as noted before, any virtue taken too far becomes a vice. Each quadrant also has a negative zone. The negative zone of Collaborate is that we have an organization that acts like a country club. The members love the organization, but not much is getting done! An organization in the negative zone of Control is a stifling bureaucracy. Slow and plodding. Almost ossified in its decision making.

An organization in the negative zone of Compete is a sweatshop. The message is always: produce, produce, produce. Employees are no more than a mere factor of production. And an organization in the negative zone of Create is a chaotic research lab. Lots of creative activity and energy, but little coordination. No closure on projects. Unpredictable outcomes.

THE CVF, LEADERSHIP, AND ORGANIZATIONAL ALIGNMENT

Leadership style is dramatically different in the four quadrants, as shown in Figure 2.4. Although all the aspects of leadership are necessary in most organizations, it is virtually impossible for any single individual to effectively play all four roles simultaneously. It may not even be advisable to try.

Focusing on one's unique strengths is preferable to trying to achieve complete balance in leadership. This is best achieved by having balance in the *management team*. That is, the leadership team should have representatives from the different quadrants. I call this "embracing the enemy" since it involves a CEO whose propensities lie in one quadrant being willing to incorporate the input of an executive from a diagonally opposite quadrant.

This is difficult to do in practice, but leaders who surrounded themselves with those from diagonally opposite quadrants have achieved great results. An example is Robert Goizueta, legendary former CEO of Coca-Cola, and his chief operating officer, Douglas Ivester. Between them they spanned all four quadrants during a time when Coca-Cola substantially strengthened its global market position.

Leader's Focus: The organization and its people **Leader's Role:** Motivator	**Leader's Focus:** The future **Leader's Role:** Vision setter
Leader's Focus: The internal operating system **Leader's Role:** Analyzer	**Leader's Focus:** The markets in which the firm operates **Leader's Role:** Taskmaster

FIGURE 2.4
The CVF and leadership style.

As we discussed before, organizational alignment is the key to successfully executing any growth strategy. Without internal alignment, one generates friction that dissipates the energy of employees and generates conflict. Without external alignment, the stock price may not reflect the true value of the company, and financiers may not provide the needed capital at attractive prices. This can slow down growth. So, alignment is essential.

The CVF can help achieve alignment. It does this by helping to simplify the description of the growth strategy. Thus, for example, Dell could have described its growth strategy as being primarily Red—driving growth through a novel supply-chain process and a relentless focus on cost productivity that enables the company to provide PCs to customers faster and at a lower cost.

By associating a color with a growth strategy, one immediately conveys *all* of the related connotations about people, the work environment and culture, the focus of leaders and leadership style, and the performance metrics. A large number of variables pertaining to organizational details linked to the growth strategy can be succinctly communicated with a single quadrant label.

Of course, simple and effective communication does not guarantee alignment, but it is a start. It provides clarity, and clarity allows people to make informed choices about whether they want to be in the game or out. Clarity helps those who choose to be in the game to focus. This focus improves the odds of organizational success. This then reduces disagreement and improves alignment. (see Figure 2.5).

LESSONS

Three key takeaways from this chapter are worth noting.

■ Despite the almost endless variety of growth strategies pursued by firms in practice, all these growth strategies can be put quite neatly into four categories. Clearly, within each category, there may be differences across firms in how they go about strategizing to achieve growth. But their strategies have more in common with each other than with the strategies pursued by firms in other

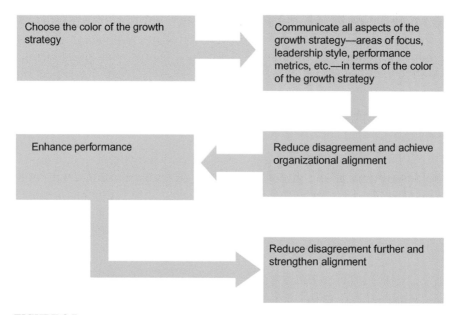

FIGURE 2.5
The color of your growth strategy.

quadrants. This has its own virtue. By being able to attach the company's growth strategy to a particular quadrant, the leader's task of communicating the strategy to the rest of the organization is greatly facilitated. The result: a better appreciation of the strategy and better alignment. We discuss this some more in Chapter 4.

- The growth strategies in the different quadrants represent *competing* forms of value creation. They pull the organization in different directions. Hence, making a choice is important for the organization. No quadrant is better than the other when it comes to growth strategy. But a choice of quadrant as the main pillar of the growth strategy is recommended.

- Despite a dominant quadrant for the growth strategy, most organizations do end up with growth strategies that span more than one quadrant. For example, Wal-Mart is both a good Red (Control) and a good Blue (Compete). This kind of spanning often generates tensions within the organization. These tensions are predicted by the CVF, so they can be recognized explicitly. That is the first step in coping with them.

Reflection Exercise

As a leader in your organization, please choose a number from 1 to 5 to assign to each statement in Exercise 2.1 on the next page. Ask the top executives in your organization to assign scores too. Take the average of the scores for each question and draw a picture based on your answers. For example, if the average scores from answers to questions (i) through (iv) are 3, 3, 4, and 2, the CVF diagram look will look like Figure 2.6.

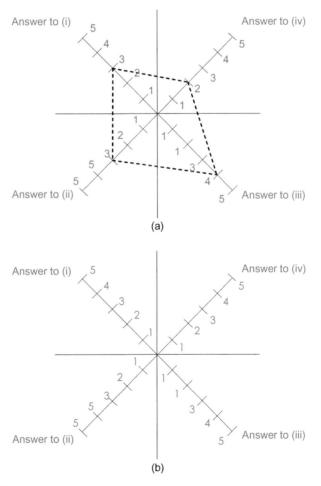

FIGURE 2.6
The growth strategy's intent.

Exercise 2.1

1 = Strongly disagree; 2 = Disagree; 3 = Neither agree nor disagree; 4 = Agree; 5 = Strongly agree

	1	2	3	4	5
(i) The principal driver of our organization's growth strategy is a deep and enduring focus on our people and our culture.	/				
(ii) What makes us distinct from other companies and powers our organization's growth is our deep commitment to our planning and other processes.					/
(iii) What positions our organization to grow is that we have a laser-sharp focus on attending to our existing markets and customers, in developing our brand equity, and/or in growing through acquisitions when necessary.			/		
(iv) The essence of our growth is our belief that we must constantly innovate and come up with new ideas for products and services.					/

- What did you learn?

- How does this help you understand the various implications of your growth strategy?

- How can this help you communicate your growth strategy and its various implications?

CHAPTER 3

The Competing Values Framework Growth Strategies and the Stock Market

> The officer of every corporation should feel in his heart—in his very soul—that he is responsible, not merely to make dividends for the stockholders of his company, but to enhance the general prosperity and the moral sentiment of the United States.
> – Adolphus Green, founder, Nabisco

Jarden Corporation grew its revenues from $305 million in 2001 to $4.7 billion in 2007. This growth earned it a spot on the *Fortune* 500 for the first time.[1] Much of this growth was achieved through the acquisition of underperforming brands. The company now markets more than 100 brands. These include many recognizable names—Sunbeam, Oster, Hoyle, Mr. Coffee, Rawlings, Crock-Pot, and First Alert.

Despite this impressive growth, however, the company's shares lost half their value during 2007–2008. Clearly, the overall decline in the stock market had a lot to do with this. Nonetheless, a declining stock price inevitably raises concerns.

A sharp contrast is provided by Kleiner Perkins Caufield & Byers, one of the top venture capital firms in Silicon Valley. The firm that bet on Genentech, Compaq, Sun, Netscape, Amazon, and Google has made billions of dollars for its investors and generated impressive returns for them.

---

[1] See *Fortune*, July 7, 2008.

29

Like it or not, it's a stock-market driven world. Those who produce handsome returns for their investors are celebrated. CEOs who don't deliver high returns are under pressure. Whether they grew profits through efficiency measures or boosted the top line through acquisitions matters little. They may make outstanding products of high quality and may have well-organized manufacturing plants equipped with the latest technology. They may have great employees. But if the firm's stock price stagnates, it is in trouble. The ultimate score card is the stock price!

So an obvious question is: How well does the Competing Values Framework (CVF) do in terms of positioning the company for *good* growth—growth that boosts the stock price?

When it comes to relating growth strategy to stock price, the CVF has to overcome the shortcomings of most measurement approaches. Most measurement devices used to assess organizational performance do not account for the tensions inherent in managing for the short run as well as the long run; or the tensions in managing predictability as well as innovation; or managing for fast payout as well as for future strength.

The CVF, on the other hand, identifies criteria of performance in each of the four quadrants, and thus incorporates these very tensions. We have conducted extensive empirical research into the relationship of the CVF with shareholder value. The findings of the research are striking:

- There is a high statistical correlation between the variables of the CVF and contemporaneous cross-sectional variations in market-to-book-value ratios of (publicly traded) companies. In other words, the CVF explains well which companies will produce the most market value for every dollar invested by their shareholders (book value).

- Investing based on the CVF also yields attractive returns. Investing in a (value-weighted) portfolio of firms that are in the top quintile based on their competing values rankings consistently yields returns that are well above market returns as well as the returns required to compensate investors for the risk they bear from investing in these top-quintile portfolios.

Quadrant	Measures for Quadrant	Proxies Used
Control	Quality Efficiency	Gross margin Asset turnover
Compete	Profit Speed	EVA Change in EVA growth
Create	Growth Innovation	Sales growth Standard deviation of the alpha based on the Capital Asset Pricing Model
Collaborate	Knowledge Community	Future growth and value of sales/number of employees

FIGURE 3.1
The proxies for the empirical tests.

DESIGNING THE EMPIRICAL TESTS

There are two types of empirical tests that we have conducted: contemporaneous and predictive.[2] Each is described below. In these tests, we assigned two variables (representing dimensions of value creation) to each of the four quadrants and then chose a proxy for each of these eight variables, as explained in Figure 3.1 .

A few words on these proxies are in order. Let us start with the Control quadrant. The two measures of value creation in this quadrant are quality and efficiency. Ideally, we would like to measure quality by directly assessing the quality of the firm's products and services.

This is, however, not feasible given the number of firms in our database. So we made the assumption that the higher the firm's product quality, the higher will be the price premium it will be able to command and thus the higher will be its *gross margin*, defined as [sales revenue minus cost of goods sold] divided by sales revenue.

As for efficiency, many measures are possible. The one I focus on is how efficiently the firm manages its asset base. I thus use the classic

---

[2]The summary here is adapted from the discussion in *Competing Values Leadership* (Kim Cameron, Jeff DeGraff, Robert Quinn, and Anjan Thakor), Edward Elgar Publishing, 2006.

definition of asset efficiency as our proxy, *asset turnover*—defined as sales—divided by assets in a given year.

Now consider the Compete quadrant, where the two measures of value creation are profit and speed. By profit, we mean *economic profit* rather than accounting net income, which is subject to all sorts of manipulations and distortions, as the events in 2002 with WorldCom, Enron, Tyco, and others have aptly illustrated. The commonly used notion of economic profit is Economic Value Added (EVA), which is defined as Net Operating Profits After Tax (NOPAT), minus a capital charge, where capital charge equals the firm's weighted-average cost of capital times Net Assets Deployed.[3]

By speed, we mean the speed with which initiatives are executed and hence economic profit is improved. We thus create a proxy for speed by the change in the firm's EVA growth rate from one year to the next, over a five-year time period.

Turning to the Create quadrant, the two measures of value creation are growth and innovation. A fairly conventional view of growth is used; it is the rate at which the company's sales are growing. Thus, the proxy for growth is sales growth.

Innovation is something we would ideally like to assess by measuring the success of the company's innovation efforts in terms of its products, services, and business designs. This is difficult to do directly given data limitations. So, an indirect approach is taken. As has been done in some recent finance research, a firm's "idiosyncratic stock return risk" is used as a proxy for its innovativeness. The idea is as follows.

A firm's stock returns are driven by two factors: its co-movement with the overall market (or economy) and its idiosyncratic circumstances. The more innovative the firm becomes, the more different it looks from the rest of the herd—the overall market. Hence, the greater is the influence of its own idiosyncratic factors in driving its stock returns relative to the influence of the overall market.

---

[3] Net Assets Deployed is typically defined as net total assets of accumulated depreciation and amortization minus noninterest-bearing current liabilities (e.g., accounts payable).

We measure idiosyncratic stock return risk by measuring the standard deviation of the firm's idiosyncratic returns—that is, the difference between its actual returns and the portion of the returns that can be explained by co-movement with overall market return. This is sometimes referred to as *alpha*.

The final quadrant is Collaborate, where the measures of value creation are knowledge and community. Organization knowledge is a highly complex variable and difficult to measure directly. So, it is better to focus on knowledge that leads to perceptions of future value creation, since the unique knowledge the organization possesses today, to the extent that it has value relevance, should lead to value creation in the future.

Thus, the proxy for knowledge is *future growth value*, which is defined as the differences between the firm's current market value (which impounds investors' expectations of future value creation) and what its market value would be if its profits (NOPAT) did not grow. That is, it is the portion of the firm's current market capitalization that is attributable to expectations about future growth. These expectations are driven by the unique knowledge assets the firm has.

As for community, what we really want to measure is one of the softest aspects of the organization: the quality of its internal community. We have the instruments with which we can do this if we were to go inside an organization and interview employees. This, however, is not possible from a database as large as the one used in this analysis.

So it is convenient to assume that the greater the impact an individual employee has on the success of the organization, the more "relevant" that employee will feel. And the greater the sense of personal relevance, the greater will be the sense of "ownership" and internal community. Thus, community is proxied by a variable defined as sales/number of employees. The more the organization sells per employee, the greater the sense of community.

These proxies are not perfect, of course, but they serve as approximations of objective financial measures in each of the quadrants. Inasmuch as publicly available financial data were used for data on these companies, these proxies are about as well as you can do.

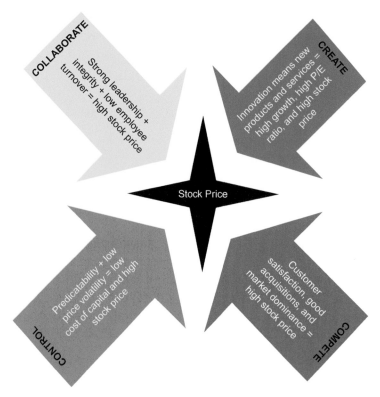

FIGURE 3.2
The CVF growth strategy and stock price.

This book's Appendix provides a summary of these proxies and the various quadrants. Figure 3.2 provides an intuitive link between the quadrants of the CVF and the firm's stock price.

Rather than focusing on the four *individual* quadrants, it is also interesting to examine how well different companies and their industries score in *all* of those quadrants. To do this, we first calculate the eight CVF performance metrics for all publicly listed companies in the United States.

We then rank these companies in each dimension by calculating a percentile score for each company in each dimension. The best performer in each dimension is assigned the maximum score of 1; the worst

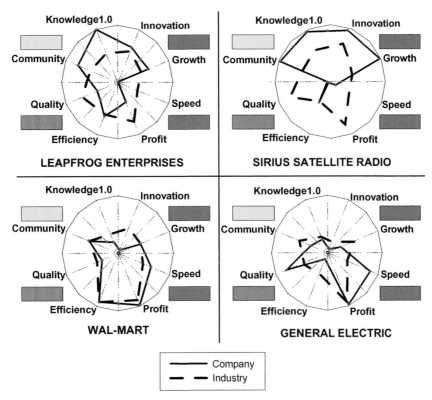

FIGURE 3.3
Selected CVF profiles.

performer receives a score of 0. The industry scores in each dimension are obtained as the average scores of all the firms in that industry.

Figure 3.3 shows CVF profiles of four companies: Leapfrog Enterprises, Sirius Satellite Radio, Wal-Mart, and General Electric. It is clear that educational toy company Leapfrog Enterprises is very strong in the Yellow quadrant and outperforms its industry both in community and in knowledge. Sirius Satellite Radio is a Yellow–Green company: It scores extremely well in community, knowledge, innovation, and growth, and by far outperforms its industry in each of those dimensions.

Wal-Mart is a Red–Blue company: It shows superb performance in the areas of efficiency and profit, respectively scoring equally well as and outperforming the general merchandise industry. General Electric is clearly a Blue company: it scores extremely high in profit and speed; while the entire industry tends to score very well on profit, GE outperforms its peers in terms of speed.

It is interesting to note that Leapfrog Enterprises and General Electric score extremely well in one quadrant, while Sirius Satellite Radio and Wal-Mart show great performance in two quadrants. Comparing the pictures, it is clear that superb performance in one quadrant is associated with mediocre performance in the diagonally opposite quadrant.

This is not a coincidence. I have examined the CVF profiles of all listed companies and have found this to be true for many companies. There are exceptions, of course. But the point is that it is hard in practice to do well in diagonally opposite quadrants.

The graphs in Figure 3.3 were created using each firm's performance in eight individual areas. It is also possible to calculate each firm's *overall* CVF ranking. We do that by calculating each firm's average score in the eight individual areas. The firm with the highest average performance in all areas is assigned the highest rank of 1; the firm with the worst average performance receives a rank of 0.

These overall CVF rankings allow us to compare the stock price performance of the highest ranking (e.g., top 20%) CVF companies with the performance of the overall market. Figure 3.4 does exactly that. It compares the performance of two portfolios: the competing values top 20% versus the stock-market portfolio.

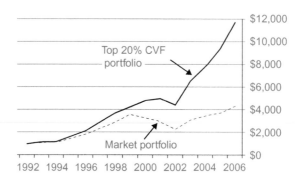

FIGURE 3.4
Stock-market performance versus CVF portfolio performance.

If investors had invested $1000 in the two portfolios on December 31, 1992, and subsequently reinvested the dividends every year until December 31, 2006, they would have fared by far the best if they had invested in the CVF portfolio. As can be seen in the figure, the competing values top 20% portfolio would be worth more than $11,500 whereas the average stock portfolio would only have increased to close to $4500.[4]

LESSONS

There are two simple lessons to be learned from this chapter.

- Using the CVF, and particularly its link to value creation and your firm's stock price, you can develop a better appreciation of your growth strategy and better alignment of the organization with this strategy.

- The CVF successfully identifies the dimensions in which a company needs to perform in order to create shareholder value. Any company that wishes to determine where its biggest bang for the buck is likely to be in terms of improving performance can use the CVF at the company level to do this. That is, the CVF can tell you what to do to get the most from your focused strategy.

In the chapters that follow, we consider various illustrations of this approach for individual companies. This can be helpful in determining the market-valuation impact of any growth strategy—a useful thing to know for any publicly traded company. And private companies can rely on the fact that if these growth strategies produce value for public firms, then they are worth considering even for private firms.

---

[4] Figure 3.4 is comparable to Figure 6.3 in *Competing Values Leadership: Creating Value in Organizations* (Cameron, Quinn, DeGraff, and Thakor, 2006). While both figures show a strong outperformance by the competing values portfolio, the dollar values do not match for two reasons. First, Figure 6.3 shows the competing values top 25% (rather than top 20%) portfolio. Second, some variable definitions (and hence competing values rankings) were changed.

Reflection Exercise

As a leader in your organization, please choose a number from 1 to 5 to assign to each statement in Exercise 3.1.

Based on your answers, create a picture like the one shown in Figure 3.5, plotting a point on each ray that corresponds to the score you gave on that dimension. Compare this to Figure 2.6, the intent of our growth strategy graph, from Chapter 2 and write down your observations about how your growth strategy intent matches up with your organizational capability to grow.

Exercise 3.1

1 = Strongly disagree; 2 = Disagree; 3 = Neither agree nor disagree; 4 = Agree; 5 = Strongly agree

	1	2	3	4	5
(i) Our organization is better than others in the industry in terms of the strength of its community.			/		
(ii) Our organization is better than others in terms of its ability to continuously generate new knowledge.				)	
(iii) Our organization is better than others in terms of its ability to innovate.		/			
(iv) Our organization is better than others in terms of its ability to grow the top line.			/		
(v) Our organization is better than others in its ability to respond quickly to market opportunities.		ǀ			
(vi) Our organization is better than others in terms of its ability to generate profits and create shareholder value.			ǀ		
(vii) Our organization is better than others because of its efficiency and planning.				ǀ	
(viii) Our organization is better than others in the quality of the products and services it provides.				/	

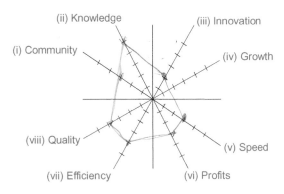

FIGURE 3.5
The capability behind our growth strategy.

CHAPTER 4

How to Know Which Color Your Growth Strategy Should Be

> In the right key one can say anything. In the wrong key, nothing:
> the only delicate part is the establishment of the key.
> – George Bernard Shaw

Anheuser-Busch InBev (formerly Anheuser-Busch) spends hundreds of millions of dollars every year on advertising, much of which is devoted to refurbishing and building its brand. Coca-Cola spends even more. Nike has built a global powerhouse on the basis of its brand. The company unveiled new footwear for athletes in all 28 sports at the 2008 Beijing Olympics, including "Ippeas" equestrian boots, which use Air Zoom cushioning. These are all Blue growth strategies that use brand development as their lifeblood.

Contrast this strategy with that of Target, which has taken an aggressive stance to compete with Wal-Mart, based on dirt-cheap prices. Its value proposition for the customer is: "Expect more, pay less." After the recession hit in 2008, the company realized that consumers were becoming more price conscious, and that Target's sales were falling.

Although its traditional strategy was to push its low-cost business model upmarket, this time Target responded by going downmarket.[1] It developed a marketing strategy in which it began to push the notion that good value can also be chic. And it expanded aggressively into groceries, a low-margin business.

---

[1] See Michelle Conlin, "Look Who's Stalking Wal-Mart," *Business Week*, December 7, 2009.

41

Moreover, it has significantly narrowed the price gap between itself and Wal-Mart. This has given the company virtual price parity with Wal-Mart, but customers may perceive the shopping experience as more upscale. Thus, Target too is following a Blue strategy, but it has a Red splash—it is focused on cost efficiency and the associated low-cost business model.

Other companies have adopted Green growth strategies, many of which also received a boost around the time of the Beijing Olympics. For example, General Electric developed a compact ultrasound machine, the LOGIQ i from GE Healthcare, a 12-pound device that can produce detailed images of even the tiniest tear in a ligament in the human body. The images have the same resolution quality as bigger machines found in hospitals. It was quite a boon for the athletes competing in the Olympics. GE had introduced an earlier version of the machine at the 2006 Winter Games in Turin, which gave the company's researchers an opportunity to try out the experiment in an environment in which extreme injuries occur quite often.

Likewise, watchmaker Omega frequently showcases new technologies at the Olympics. In Beijing in 2008, the company introduced motion sensors (to spot false starts) and global positioning satellite systems (to track rowers).[2] (See Figure 4.1.)

So we have different companies following growth strategies with different colors. The question is: What color should your growth strategy be? That's what we will discuss in this chapter.

THE SEVEN-STEP STRATEGY FORMULATION PROCESS

Step 1: Understand "What's a Growth Strategy?"

A growth strategy is a process of identifying a key *value driver* (linked to your core competence) that resources can then be allocated to in order to drive revenue and growth in *all* parts of the business. It determines

---

[2] See *Business Week*, August 18, 2008.

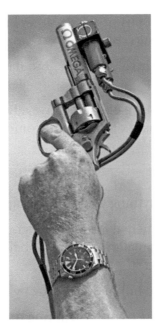

FIGURE 4.1
In 2008, Omega, the official Olympic timekeeper since 1932, linked the starting gun to loudspeakers at each starting block. That way, all runners hear the "pop!" simultaneously.

the opportunities you pursue and your tolerance for risk. That is, it is an essential guide for resource allocation, for focusing organizational efforts, and for decision making.

Step 2: Define Value Driver—What It Is

- Something you can manage with your *core competence* that enables the organization to succeed in a business that then drives the success of the rest of the organization.
- A shorthand way to think about this is to think of a value driver as the *lead steer* business or the one business whose success is critical to the success of the whole organization.
  - If the value-driver business succeeds, so do the other businesses in the organization.

- If the value-driver business fails, other businesses do not have much chance to succeed.

- You can have multiple value drivers (but have the discipline not to exceed three).

- A value driver is a source of competitive advantage if managed well, and it's the determinant of success outcomes.

Step 3: Value Driver—Understand What It Is Not

- A laundry list of everything you think is important to succeed.

- An external environmental factor (demographics, geopolitics, the macro economy, population growth, global warming, etc.) that you cannot control.

- An outcome (e.g. $10 billion in revenue by 2015).

- Something you can focus on by ignoring the rest of your business (e.g., ignoring a value driver can kill you, but focusing on a value driver does not mean you can ignore your other businesses).

Step 4: Develop a Shared Understanding of Core Competence

- A core competence is a bundle of skills and technologies that yield a fundamental customer benefit. (See Figure 4.2.)

Step 5: What Is a Core Competence?

It's a good idea to put every core competence candidate through a test. A capability is a core competence if and only if the answer to each of the six questions that follow is "yes":

- Is it widely held throughout the organization?

- Is it difficult to imitate?

- Does it make a disproportionate contribution to customer perceived value or produce a substantial cost savings?

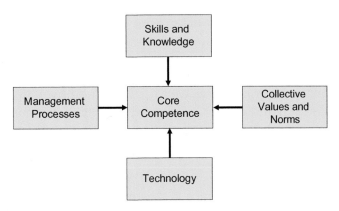

FIGURE 4.2
Core competence.

- ☒ Are we better at it than our competence competitors?

- ☒ Is the competence critical to our present position?

- ☒ Does the competence provide potential access to a wide variety of markets?

Step 6: Use Examples of Value Drivers and Strategies

What other organizations have used can sharpen your understanding. In the mid-1980s, Howard Schultz started Starbucks. The backdrop for his new venture was the United States's coffee industry, which was essentially a commodity business by 1988. That year, General Foods lost $40 million on its domestic coffee business. And Proctor & Gamble, the market-share leader, was faced with vanishing profit margins. Why did Starbucks succeed when major players like General Foods, Proctor & Gamble (P&G), and Nestlé failed?

The main reason is that Starbucks chose a different value driver from the one picked by those who dominated the coffee business in the 1980s. General Foods, P&G, and Nestlé viewed their value drivers as essentially Red: low cost (price), national brands, and mass distribution. Starbucks, by contrast, viewed its key value driver as essentially Blue: superior-quality coffee (as perceived by the customer) sold in cafés close to people's place of work and the whole experience of consuming European-style coffee in a café.

Michael Eisner took over as CEO of Walt Disney & Company in September 1984, replacing the CEO at the time, Ron Miller. Over the next 15 years, the company delivered shareholder returns in excess of 20% per year. How did Eisner do it? He did it by identifying a Green core competence—Disney's creativity. The value driver through which this core competence was expressed was Disney's film business.

The strategy then was to focus primarily on film rather than Disney's other businesses—theme parks, real estate, and consumer products.

FIGURE 4.3
DVD covers of popular Disney movies.

Company	Core Competence	Value Drivers	Strategy
Disney (Eisner)	– Creativity	– Film	– Get back to basics and make 16 films per year (1984) – Green
Starbucks	– Knowledge of coffee business and upscale professionals – Access to key coffee-bean suppliers	– New mode of making and selling high-quality coffee – Lack of competition from majors	– Establish cafés close to places of work to sell high-quality coffee – Blue
Citicorp (under John Reed)	– Global reach and a global customer brand	– Global growth in personal wealth and consumer banking opportunities – Corporate globalization	– Establish a global consumer bank with "model" Citi branches, and target corporate customers with international brand names and franchises – Blue
HSBC	– Knowledge of numerous local banking markets worldwide	– Global presence and nascent brand	–The world's local bank – Blue

FIGURE 4.4
Examples of value drivers and strategies.

The idea was not to ignore these other businesses; rather, it was to recognize that their success would be driven in large part by Disney's ability to create blockbuster movies (see Figure 4.3) that would then provide the characters for the theme parks and consumer products.

Value drivers differ from firm to firm, but the fact remains that strategy must be anchored by them. The color of the value driver determines the color of the strategy. It is the company's core competence that determines the color of the firm's value driver (see Figure 4.4).

Step 7: Develop a Simple Strategy Statement and Communicate, Communicate, and Communicate

Go to a company of your choice and ask: "Can you tell me what your growth strategy is?" You are likely to get one of three kinds of responses. One is a bland statement that mentions everything and says nothing. Something like: "Our strategy is to be good to the environment, delight our customers, and produce substantial value for our shareholders."

That's wonderful. But such a statement does little to help achieve organizational alignment for the key resource allocation decisions the company needs to make. This is because it doesn't tell you *how* the company plans to grow and create value. It doesn't provide a road map for *where* the company wants to go. It doesn't provide guidance to managers about where to allocate scarce resources. It doesn't tell managers which project ideas to accept and which to say no to. These are all things that a good growth strategy is supposed to do.

In short, *a growth strategy is a roadmap for how the company will make resource allocation decisions in order to achieve its growth targets.* Moreover, a good growth strategy should be a roadmap for "good" or value-enhancing growth—this is growth that leads to returns on net assets exceeding the company's cost of capital (see Chapter 1).

If you don't get this response, you may receive something like a 30-page document. Something that is chockfull of tactical details about marketing plans, specific new product ideas, capital investment plans, and so on. While such a document is informative, the problem is that it is a poor substitute for a succinct strategy statement.

Few managers will refer to a 30-page document to decide where to allocate resources. Such documents are not terribly useful as growth strategy statements. Moreover, the excessive level of detail makes it difficult to effectively communicate to develop organizational alignment.

A third response you might get is a succinct, meaningful statement of growth strategy, one that satisfies the criteria described above. We will see various examples in this chapter of companies with powerful growth strategies that can be succinctly expressed like this.

A good growth strategy statement must satisfy the five conditions that follow:

1. It must be simple, so that everybody in the organization can understand it, relate to it, and internalize their role in executing it. A good strategy statement must have a "two-minute" sound byte that captures its essence. That way employees will not have to refer to a manual every time they want to know what the company's strategy is.

2. It must clearly define what the company will do and what it will *not* do. There are far too may flowery (and very wordy) statements

of corporate growth strategy that are conspicuously silent about what they commit the corporation to *not* do. They are not worth much. The goal of a good strategy must be to guide corporate resource allocation. As a wise observer once said, "Having a strategy means being able to say no to good ideas."

3. It must be clearly tied to the key *value drivers* in the business.

4. It must focus on *how* value will be created rather than on the *outcomes* of value creation (like profits or returns on assets).

5. It should be time bound and specific. It must differ enough from competitors' strategies to give the company a distinctive competitive advantage.

A great example of a good growth strategy is provided by Michael Eisner's articulation of it when he took over as Disney CEO in 1984 (see also Figure 4.4):

> We'll get back to basics and focus on film. Judge me on one thing and one thing alone. We'll make 16 films next year.

This strategy statement (details excluded) satisfies all of the conditions identified here. It would be useful for you to think about how it does that.

Once a good growth strategy has been articulated, two crucial steps remain.

Two More Steps

The first step is to make sure that the organization is *aligned* behind the strategy. This alignment has the following three key components:

1. Resource allocation and acquisition decisions that support the strategy.

2. The performance metrics by which a project's people and business units are judged in order to execute the strategy.

3. The people and organizational culture behind the strategy.

That is, if Disney's growth strategy is to focus on making more films, then its process for the allocation of human and financial capital has to enable the organization to make more films.

Moreover, if the organization wants to engage in making more films, then performance metrics, as well as the people and organization culture, have to reward the activities that facilitate that strategic imperative. The culture that goes with, say, a Green strategy is different from one that goes with a Red strategy.

I call this relationship between growth strategy, resource allocation and acquisition, performance metrics, and people and organizational culture the *value sphere* (see Figure 4.5), where the growth strategy can be Yellow, Red, Blue, or Green.[3]

The second step is to make sure that the strategy is communicated clearly to the organization—repeatedly. Organizational leaders often

FIGURE 4.5

The value sphere of a growth strategy.

---

[3] See *The Value Sphere* by John Boquist, Todd Milbourn, and Anjan V. Thakor, VIA Press, 2006.

under-communicate the organization's growth strategy by a factor of 5 or 10! In the next chapter, we will discuss in detail *how* to use the CVF to communicate effectively. That is, we come back to Step 7 of the seven-step strategy formulation process. This step is critically important for successful strategy execution.

LESSONS

There are four key takeaways from this chapter.

- Identify your core competence and the associated key value driver—what it is, what its color is, and how it is related to your organization's core competence.

- Develop a growth strategy anchored by this value driver. The color of the value driver influences the dominant color of your growth strategy. Create a simple statement (two bullet points) of the strategy.

- Align the organization with the growth strategy—the resource allocation and acquisition, the performance metrics, and the people and organizational culture.

- Communicate the strategy at every opportunity . . . over and over again.

Reflection Exercise

As a leader in your organization, please first fill in the blanks in (i) through (iii). Then have various groups within the organization enter a score for items (i) through (iv).

Each person should choose a number from 1 to 5 to assign to each statement in Exercise 4.1.

Exercise 4.1 1 = Strongly disagree; 2 = Disagree; 3 = Neither agree nor disagree; 4 = Agree; 5 = Strongly agree	1	2	3	4	5
(i) Everybody in our organization would agree that our core competence is _____. (Fill in the blank.)					
(ii) Everybody in our organization would agree that the key value driver associated with this core competence is _____ _____ _____ _____ (Fill in the blank.)					
(iii) Everybody in our organization would agree that our strategy is _____. _____ _____ (Write it in two to three sentences.)					
(iv) Our resource allocation and acquisition, performance metrics, and people and organizational culture are aligned with our strategy.					

As an additional exercise, do the following:

- Ask various levels in the organization to go through the same exercise.

- Compare average scores across the different levels.

- What does this exercise reveal?

Alignment for Growth: The CVF's Power in Aligning Organizations through a Common Language

> These are our stories. They tell us who we are.
> — Anthwara to Picard, TNG/"Journey's End"
> in *Quotable Star Trek* by Jill Sherwin

Today, we take it for granted that we, *Homo sapiens*, represent the only hominid on this planet. Yet many different hominid species shared the planet for at least 4 million years.[1] A few hundred thousand years ago, a hominid species that had a lot in common with us occupied most of Europe and western Asia. Called *Neanderthals*, these hominids were the most accomplished practitioners of "prepared-core" tool technology—such as the hand axe—on earth until *Homo sapiens* arrived in Europe about 40,000 years ago.

From the exhibit at the Neanderthal Museum in Krapina, Croatia.

---

[1] See Ian Tattersall, "Once We Were Not Alone," *Scientific American*, January 2000, pp. 56–62. I use the term "hominids" to refer to humans and relatives of humans closer than chimpanzees. That is, it refers to the family of humans, Hominidae, which consists of all species on the human side of the last common ancestor of humans and living apes.

53

The innovation of prepared-core technology was part of a process of intermittent technological change among hominid species over millions of years. The first recognizable stone tools appeared in the archeological record from about 2.5 million years ago. This innovation was a major cognitive leap forward for hominids, and was followed by a long period of apparently no further technological breakthroughs.

It was another million years or so before the hand axe was invented. This design remained unchanged for another million years, until the invention of "prepared-core" tools. This involved a stone core that was elaborately shaped in such a way that a single blow would detach a finished implement. Prepared-core tools significantly speeded up enhancements in the original hand axe, and it became possible to use these tools to design and build a variety of new implements and weapons for hunting.

Neanderthals became masters at the practice of prepared-core technology. In many respects Neanderthals were similar to humans. Actually equipped with larger brain cavities than humans, they too lived together in small social groups, cared for those in the group, were hunter-gatherers, and refined the tools they needed for hunting.

Despite this and the fact that they had adapted to and survived the ice age in Europe for millennia, Neanderthals vanished completely from the face of the earth about 30,000 years ago. That's a mere 10,000 years after *Homo sapiens* arrived in Europe. The conjecture is that the extinction of Neanderthals so soon after the arrival of *Homo sapiens* was more than a mere coincidence.

A fascinating question for those who do research in this area is: why did Neanderthals become extinct? If there is a causal link between the arrival of *Homo sapiens* and the disappearance of Neanderthals, what relative evolutionary advantages possessed by *Homo sapiens* allowed them to triumph in such spectacular fashion?

Although the experts don't all agree on this, one compelling hypothesis that has been put forth is that humans had a capacity that was born in the proximity of the origin of the *Homo sapiens* species. This capacity lay dormant until it was activated by a cultural stimulus of some sort. And, once activated, it spread rapidly by cultural contact among human populations.

What was this cultural stimulus? The best bet at this stage appears to be the invention of *language*. This invention offered numerous advantages. First, it permitted effective communication both within and among separate human tribes or groups. This facilitated *alignment*. Especially when it came to aligning against a common foe—say another hominid species like the Neanderthals.

Moreover, language is not only the medium by which we express ideas to each other. It is fundamental to the *thought process* itself. That is, language alters thought. In fact, it is virtually impossible to conceive of thought in the absence of language since it is language that allows us to categorize and name objects and make associations between them. So the second advantage of language is that it allowed *Homo sapiens* to elevate their thought processes.

Third, the elevation of thought led to the emergence of symbolic thinking—art, carvings, cave paintings, and so on. And this led eventually to the development of more sophisticated hunting and fishing tools and techniques.

Reconstruction of a Neanderthal child from *http://en.wikipedia.org/wiki/Gibraltar*. Courtesy of Anthropological Institute, University of Zürich.

But fourth, and perhaps most important, language allowed early *Homo sapiens* to communicate their technological breakthroughs *across* tribes, so that a useful innovation did not remain localized but spread across different groups. That is, there were diverse technological experiments in different groups, but the groups communicated with each other. The consequence?

The pattern of intermittent technological innovation that had characterized hominid species for millions of years was gone. In its place was *constant* refinement. The Neanderthals had no chance to compete against this. They lacked the language, the symbolic thinking, and the constant innovation.

THE POWER OF A COMMON LANGUAGE

Just as a common language gave early humans a powerful competitive advantage over Neanderthals, it can also give a country or an organization a powerful competitive advantage. As we have seen, a language does four important things:

1. It helps to achieve *alignment*.

2. It changes how people *think*.

3. It permits many complex issues to be simplified and expressed in *symbolic terms*.

4. It allows local innovations to be more rapidly communicated across small groups, thereby facilitating *constant innovation*.

In organizations, a fundamental challenge leaders face is *alignment*. How do you get everybody aligned behind the growth strategy? How do you get a diverse workforce to all buy into the strategy?

If you don't think this is an important problem, do a focus group of, say, 30 executives in any (especially large) organization (see Figure 5.1).

FIGURE 5.1
Saudi Arabian Ministry of Higher Education leaders discussing how to get a diverse workforce aligned behind a growth strategy.

Break them up into, say, six groups of five executives each. Give them the following assignment:

> Write down the key value driver for your organization, and then write down a two-bullet–point statement of your growth strategy that is anchored by that value driver.

Bring the executives back together and see whether all groups report the same thing. If they do, you have alignment. But don't be discouraged if you don't. In my experience, it is not common to find alignment. And the larger the group you assemble, the greater the divergence of opinions will be.

Not having alignment on strategy is costly. Some of the consequences may be:

- Loss of employee motivation
- Employees exhibiting declining confidence in leaders
- Misallocation of resources because resource-allocation decisions are not aligned with growth strategy
- Too many arguments about whether specific projects and initiatives are worth pursuing, which dissipates energy and frustrates employees

What the Competing Values Framework (CVF) provides is a simple common language with which to:

- Communicate the growth strategy and achieve *alignment*
- Focus the *thinking* of the organization on the key value driver and how this value driver is the key to growth
- Help express the organization's many complex priorities in the *symbolic* four colors of the framework, thus helping to simplify and *focus* its resources and energy
- Provide a simple common language with which employees can communicate their ideas for innovations in all aspects of the business, thereby facilitating *constant innovation*

When the Power of a Common Language Is the Greatest

A common language is always helpful. But there are some circumstances in which it is most useful. The circumstances in which its power is the follow.

When There Is Complexity

One circumstance is when there is a very large variety of organizational issues to deal with, and this results in bewildering complexity. Many organizations are faced with numerous priorities and challenges (see Figure 5.2). These often seem complex and disconnected. People find it hard to cope with them all. The consequence? Confusion and a loss of energy.

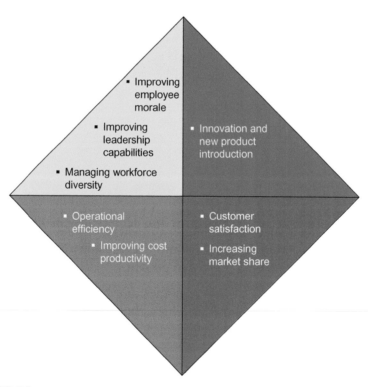

FIGURE 5.2
Complex priorities create organizational tensions.

In these busy and challenging times, a major challenge for most organizations is keeping people's (positive) energy up. A typical large organization might state its key priorities as:

- Improving employee morale

- Improving the leadership capabilities of key employees

- Customer satisfaction

- Operational efficiency

- Innovation and new product introduction

- Improving cost productivity

- Improving product quality

- Increasing market share

- Managing workforce diversity

At first blush, this seems quite reasonable. Every priority is a virtue of sorts. So why not ask the organization to focus on all of them?

But now plot these in CVF space.

Look at the priorities now. As the CVF tells us, they will tend to pull employees and the organization in opposite directions. Unless there is a way to recognize and reconcile these seemingly conflicting priorities, employees will experience these tensions and be less productive than they could be. This organization has two choices.

One is to cut back on some priorities in order to reduce the potential conflicts among the priorities. The other is to explain to the employees where the potential tensions might be and how the organization intends to deal with them. The CVF is enormously useful in this exercise. The larger the number of priorities, the greater is the potential for conflicts among them. Hence, the greater is the potential for *dilution* of focus. And thus the greater is the power of a common language that simplifies, clarifies, and achieves true *focus*.

When It Creates a Stronger Sense of Community

Often, an organization will use language to unify its own people and differentiate the organization from others. Quite often this is done

Table 5.1 Real Organizations' Acronyms and Definitions	
Acronym	**Definition**
DCF	Dominant Consumer Franchise
DCF	Discounted Cash Flow
RONA	Return on Net Assets
ROTCE	Return on Total Capital Employed
MIN	Materials Information Network
OPEX	Operational Excellence
ROI	Return on Investment
TCP	Total Cost Productivity
OCE	Office of the Chief Executive
GEX	Global Executive Committee
EXCO	Executive Committee
GM	Gross Margin
EVA	Economic Value Added
DCFROI	Discounted Cash Flow Return on Investment
NOPAT	Net Operating Profit After Tax
CFROGI	Cash Flow Return on Gross Investment

through *acronyms*. Some are generally used acronyms whose meanings are fairly commonly known. Others are company-specific. The meanings of these are known only to "insiders"—those who have been around for a while. It is not uncommon to get a blizzard of acronyms. The ones listed in Table 5.1 are a few examples from real organizations.

I was once working with a company that had so many acronyms that it was going to take me a while to learn them all. At one point, I was doing an executive development program with about 40 managers and decided to "get even." So I made up my own acronym and casually slipped it into my conversation, mentioning it a couple of times. No one asked me what it was. I guess no one wanted to admit to not being an "insider." But during the next break, someone walked up to me and inquired sheepishly about the acronym. He was sure he had heard it before, but just couldn't remember it!

While acronyms can be amusing—and sometimes downright funny—they also serve a (possibly unintended) purpose. Organizations often develop a sense of "proprietary ownership" of their acronyms, and this helps create a unified sense of community. Pretty much the same way that every generation develops its own slang that previous generations did not use—like "groovy," "cool," "bad" (to indicate really good), and so on.

It's a way of creating a group identity and is the same with any other unifying language that creates a sense of identity for the organization.

When Diversity of People Grows

The world of business is becoming increasingly diverse. Leaders with diverse viewpoints and economic agendas are emerging all over the world. For example, in its May 14, 2007, issue, *Time* magazine listed its 100 most influential people in the world. And these included Michael Bloomberg, Sonia Gandhi, Hu Jintao, Hillary Clinton, and Liu Qi.

Increasing diversity in any organization (or country) has the enormous benefit of bringing a variety of fresh perspectives into play. But there is also a downside. Diversity can work against unity. It can work against alignment.

In fact, as the world becomes increasingly diverse and yet increasingly connected, we see a greater yearning for communication and community. This is evident in social networks such as Twitter and Facebook. It is also evident in the emergence of technologies such as SixthSense and other digital interfaces.

SixthSense technology, invented by Pranav Mistry, an Indian graduate student at MIT, allows the elimination of keyboards so that commands to computers can be communicated via hand gestures and the like. It is a "wearable gestural interface" that allows us to augment the physical world around us with digital information and then use natural hand gestures to interact with that information.

In fact, the technology even permits eliminating monitors, as the whole world around you becomes your computer! It will enable an explosion in new ways to communicate in the years to come. Such changes will allow diverse communities all over the world to talk to each other in forms that may be difficult to imagine right now.

Similarly, a common language helps take advantage of diversity without fracturing the organization. Using the CVF, different perspectives can be mapped into the four quadrants. The virtue of each perspective can then be appreciated. And the inevitable tensions can be recognized and dealt with constructively.

When to Measure Things We Cannot See or Touch

There are many things happening around us that we experience but cannot touch or see. For example, we experience national pride, but we cannot see or touch it on any given day. We may, to our chagrin, eventually experience the effect of high cholesterol. But it can't be seen or touched.

Such intangible phenomena are often more important than the things we can touch and see. *Corporate culture* is an example in the case of

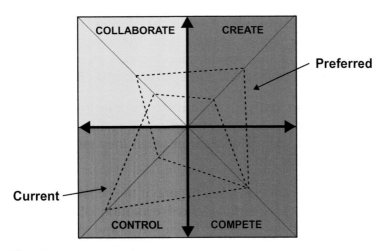

FIGURE 5.3
Current and preferred culture profiles.

organizations. Nobody denies it is important. But it's difficult to define it. It's difficult to give it tangible form. It's difficult to know how to shape it so that it can be aligned with the organization's growth strategy.

The CVF provides a language that helps us assess organizational culture. Using a culture diagnostic instrument,[2] we can actually "measure" the current culture of the organization as well as its preferred culture. The assessment is done by asking selected groups of people within the organization a series of questions about behaviors, metrics, goals, and priorities, and then aggregating the data. An example of such an exercise is shown in Figure 5.3.

The culture profiles shown in the figure indicate that the organization wishes to make its culture more Yellow and Green and less Red. Once this is established, there is a discussion of whether such a cultural evolution is compatible with the organization's growth strategy. One can presume that, in the case of this organization, the growth strategy depends on an increased focus on innovation and more organic growth through new products.

---

[2] See Kim Cameron and Robert Quinn, *Diagnosing and Changing Corporate Culture*. San Francisco: Jossey-Bass, 2006.

The next step is to discuss what it means to be more Yellow and more Green. There are no canned answers here. The behavioral and other changes needed to make one organization more Green may be quite different from those needed to make some other organization more Green.

It is just as important to discuss what it means to be less Red and what it does *not* mean. For example, no organization I know wants to be *less* efficient—that's not what people mean when they say they want the organization to be less Red.

Out of these discussions emerges a picture of the behavioral and other changes needed to achieve the desired evolution of organizational culture. Most importantly, there is often a rich and clarifying discussion of individual and organizational behaviors needed to successfully implement the growth strategy.

We can put this in perspective as follows. If you are growing, you are moving. The CVF serves as a change management tool to help clarify *where* you are today (Point A) and where your growth will take you (Point B). You want your organizational culture to support your growth strategy, and having a roadmap for cultural clarity is critical. It is this roadmap that the CVF provides.

Another key issue that emerges from this exercise is *leadership development*. A clear culture map can help define your leadership development strategy—a strategy whereby your leaders engage in the behaviors that support your growth strategy.

LESSONS

There are three key things to take away from this chapter.

- Find a way to communicate your growth strategy in simple, vivid terms, so all stakeholders can internalize it. A simple language like the one provided by the CVF can help in crafting a simple statement of strategy.

- A common language has the power to clarify in the face of complexity; align in the face of diversity; speed up communication across disparate groups; and stimulate innovation. This is just as true for organizations today as it was for the early *Homo sapiens* who displaced Neanderthals 30,000 years ago.

■ Use the common simple language of the CVF to diagnose your current organizational culture. Use it to clarify the preferred culture that will help you execute your growth strategy.

Reflection Exercise

As a leader in your organization, please choose a number from 1 to 5 to assign to each statement in Exercise 5.1.

Exercise 5.1
1 = Strongly disagree; 2 = Disagree; 3 = Neither agree nor disagree; 4 = Agree; 5 = Strongly agree

	1	2	3	4	5
(i) Our organization has a great deal of complexity.					
(ii) Our organization could benefit from a better sense of community.					
(iii) Our organization has a great deal of diversity.					
(iv) We could benefit from a clearer identification of our organizational culture and an examination of its alignment with our growth strategy.					

■ What did you learn? This exercise should help guide the assessment of your organization's need for a common language.

CHAPTER 6

Ideas for Yellow Growth Strategies

The best soldier does not attack. The superior fighter succeeds without violence. The greatest conqueror wins without a struggle. The most successful manager leads without dictating. This is called intelligent nonaggressiveness. This is called mastery of men.
— Lao-Tzu, Tao Te Ching, taken from *Unlimited Power* by Anthony Robbins

There is a small town in the Colorado Rockies called Estes Park. Located there is a small Italian restaurant called Sweet Basilico, which serves truly great food. But what also distinguishes the restaurant is an exceptionally warm and friendly owner (who is also the head chef). He greets customers personally, talks to many, and has a staff that reflects his friendly, service-oriented approach. It's a very "Yellow" place! This restaurant has grown explosively in the past few years. So much so that the owner has moved the business to a bigger place in a different location. All this with zero advertising.

Go to any Disney theme park. Go to any restaurant in the park. If you have the misfortune of having something go wrong—say the server spills a soft drink on you—the staff will immediately respond by doing *three* nice things for you! The theme park staff is trained to make customers happy. And they are also made to feel like they are part of a giant theatrical production that must run flawlessly. They are not referred to as employees. Rather, they are "cast members."

There is an airline in India called Jet Airways. Take any domestic flight, any time, for any duration, and you'll experience superior customer service. If you are used to the kind of service one typically gets flying coach on any U.S. or European carrier, you will be blown away. Jet Airways has an extremely friendly crew that is eager to be of service. The Yellow part of the culture shows! Flights depart on time; bags don't get mishandled; and a hot meal is served on even short hops of less than an hour's duration. In coach! Jet Airways has grown rapidly and now flies in and out of the United States and Europe as well.

Like a growth strategy of any other color, a Yellow growth strategy is designed to ultimately improve the effectiveness of the organization in reaching customers—old and new—and improving its value creation. But perhaps unlike the other growth strategies, it is all about getting *people* to achieve their *highest* potential.

HOW TO BECOME A BETTER YELLOW

It is difficult for many organizations to sustain a higher performance culture—in part because nobody has the time to focus on it. But there are specific tools to achieve this. The "abundance approach" is one such tool. It is a part of what has been called "Positive Leadership."[1] It is an approach being increasingly used by many high-performance organizations. Every West Point cadet being trained for the U.S. military is now taught this. It is exemplified by the following quotation:

> As a leader . . . You have an obligation to develop a positive attitude, one that inspires the people around you to achieve the impossible. Great leaders possess a passion for their causes. If enough people care, there isn't any problem in the world we can't solve.
> **– Lou Holtz in *Winning Every Day***

What is the abundance approach? To understand it, let us first consider the standard approach to organizational change—the "problem-solving

---

[1] See Kim Cameron, *Positive Leadership: Strategies for Extraordinary Performance*, Berrett-Koehler Publishers, Inc., San Francisco, 2008.

approach." This approach says that the way one addresses a situation is to:

- Identify the problem
- Perform a root-cause analysis
- Identify solutions
- Plan actions/interventions to address or solve the problem

The basic assumption is that as leaders our job is to overcome major problems and challenges.

By contrast, the abundance approach says that as organization leaders we should:

- Identify, appreciate, and celebrate peak experiences
- Explain success by identifying the elements of the best past successes
- Create sustainability by identifying what should be continued in the future
- Design interventions that create an ideal future

The basic assumption is that our job as leaders is to embrace and enable the highest potential of those in the organization.

An *abundance gap* is defined as the gap between the highest level of excellence and performing at a normal level. It's the difference between Mahatma Gandhi and a demonstrator at a political rally; the difference between Michael Jordan and a recreational basketball player; or the difference between Berkshire Hathaway and a profitable firm.

Thus, while our usual approach is to focus on *deficit gaps*—going from being unprofitable to being profitable—by solving problems, the abundance approach seeks to reach higher. It is aimed at taking individuals and organizations from being good to being exceptional.

At this point, you're probably thinking: "Yeah, but . . .

- Aren't most organizations fraught with problems?

- Can any sane leader or manager afford to ignore difficulties?

- Is a positive approach to change just a whitewash of serious challenges?

- Won't any business fail if it neglects to focus on its weaknesses and liabilities?

- In light of the major challenges faced by most organizations and by most leaders, what is the relevance of a virtues or abundance approach to change?"

Well, I wouldn't blame you. It is human nature to focus more on the negatives. And also to be suspicious of prescriptions to focus on the positives.

WHY POSITIVE FACTORS DON'T GET MORE ATTENTION

A systematic bias exists in people that shows that negative factors are more powerful than positive factors.

- People are more affected by one traumatic or negative event than by one positive or happy event (for example, losing $1000 compared to winning $1000).

- People are more affected emotionally and do more mental work from a single negative piece of feedback than from a single positive piece of feedback.

- Evolutionary theory suggests why: If people ignore negative information, it could cost them their lives. Think of all the species that ignored the roar of a lion or the hiss of a cobra. They became extinct! If people ignore positive feedback, it only causes regret.

- Therefore, it is not surprising that negative phenomena get more attention than positive phenomena. It takes conscious effort to adopt an abundance approach.

The irony, however, is this. Adopting an abundance approach—enabling the best of the human condition, displaying virtuous behaviors, unleashing human thriving—has inherent value. We think of this as fundamentally the right thing to do. Virtually all cultures are based upon the same inherent goodness.

On the other hand, if an observable, bottom-line impact is not connected to an abundance approach, it becomes ignored in favor of the very real pressures of improving organizational effectiveness. Pressures like delivering higher returns to shareholders, increasing profitability, improving productivity, and enhancing customer satisfaction. If virtuousness doesn't pay, it is ignored in business.

The fact of the matter is that abundance does work. Research has shown that organizations that practice abundance also exhibit high performance.[2] The research involved a study of 60 top management teams who were engaged in annual strategic-planning, problem-solving, and budget-setting activities.[3] The goal of the research was to find out why some management teams performed better than others.

Teams of senior managers who worked together on a regular basis were put in three performance categories: high, medium, or low. The way they were performance categorized was based on the performance of their organization: profitability, customer satisfaction, and 360-degree evaluations of the managers who were included in the teams. Of the 60 teams, 15 were rated as high, 26 as medium, and 19 as low in their performance.

The teams were studied on the basis of their communication patterns. These patterns of team members were monitored during the workday and put into four communication categories by trained raters. The raters were unaware of the performance level of the teams. The communication categories used were the ratio of *positive* to *negative* comments, the ratio of *inquiry* to *advocacy* comments, the ratio of a

---

[2] See M. Losada and E.D. Heaphy, "Positivity and Connectivity," *American Behavioral Scientist* 47 (6), 2004, pp. 740–765.

[3] See Losada and Heaphy (2004).

	TEAM PERFORMANCE		
	High	Medium	Low
Positive Statement Ratio (supportive, encouraging, appreciation versus critical disapproval, contradictory)	5.6 to 1	1.8 to 1	0.36 to 1
Inquiry/Advocacy Ratio (questioning versus asserting)	1.1 to 1	0.67 to 1	0.05 to 1
Others/Self Ratio (external versus internal focus)	0.94 to 1	0.62 to 1	0.03 to 1
Connectivity Average (mutual influence, assistance, interaction)	32	22	18

FIGURE 6.1
Communication in top management teams.

focus on *others* to a focus on *self*, and a measure of *connectivity*, or the amount of interaction, engagement, and information exchanged in the team.

The most important factor in predicting organizational performance was the ratio of positive statements to negative statements. Positive statements express appreciation, support, helpfulness, approval, or compliments. Negative statements include criticism, disapproval, dissatisfaction, cynicism, or disparagement.

Look at Figure 6.1, which summarizes the results of the study. It shows that in high-performing organizations, the ratio of positive to negative statements in their top management teams was 5.6 to 1. In medium-performing organizations, the ratio was 1.85 to 1. In low-performing organizations, the ratio was 0.36 to 1.

Team members in high-performing organizations were found to be balanced in the number of *inquiry* statements (i.e., asking questions, seeking others' viewpoints) compared to *advocacy* statements (i.e., telling, or advocating, a position), whereas low-performing organizations were highly overloaded toward advocacy rather than inquiry.

High performers had a ratio of 1.1 inquiries for every 1.0 advocacy statements. Low performers had a ratio of 0.05 to 1, or 5 inquiries for every 100 advocacy statements. A relative balance also existed in the focus on *self* versus *others*.

The obvious first reaction to these findings is: "Wait a minute! Isn't it easier for leaders in well-performing organizations to send positive messages than it is for leaders in poorly performing organizations?" True. But this study was careful to use the appropriate statistical technique to check for the direction of causality. It turns out that there is in fact a *causal* relationship between positive communication and high performance.

These findings show that high-performing organizations had communication patterns that were significantly more positive than those of low-performing organizations. In fact, about 15.5 times more positive!

This does *not* mean that Pollyanna-like behavior leads to high performance. Research has shown that a positive-to-negative communication ratio of between 3 and 9 predicts the highest levels of performance.[4] High-performance organizations do *not* avoid negative communication—after all, the ratio of positive to negative communication is 5.6 to 1, suggesting that roughly one out of every seven communications is negative. Moreover, once the ratio gets too high (above 10), effectiveness is lost.

I can illustrate this with a personal experience. I had once advised a senior leader in an organization to practice the positive communication aspect of abundance and pick two or three people to recognize and thank for their achievements. He took my advice. At the next meeting he had with a group, he started by applauding the achievements of a couple of people.

Those people were surprised and visibly pleased. He then moved on to the third person to recognize. There was considerable positive energy in the room. But he didn't stop there. He went on to thank each and every person in the room. As the set of people being recognized grew, the positive energy in the room ebbed as well. Essentially, the positive communication was rendered virtually meaningless by the excessive nature of it.

---

[4] See B.S. Frederickson and M.F. Losada, "Positive Affect and the Complex Dynamics of Human Flourishing," *American Psychologist* 60, 2005, pp. 678–686.

BEYOND ABUNDANCE—OTHER ASPECTS OF A YELLOW CULTURE AND GROWTH STRATEGY

At its core, a Yellow growth strategy is based on three principles: employee engagement, integration, and teamwork. In this sense, one can think of Yellow as *enhancing* a growth strategy of any other color. It is a cultural orientation that wraps around any growth strategy and gives it legs.

To see the power of employee engagement, integration, and teamwork— all of which are fueled by an abundance approach—think of the McKinsey and Ericsson examples in Chapter 2. In the case of McKinsey, these elements help with employee retention and more effective customer relationships. This leads to growth. In the case of Ericsson, it helps to generate knowledge assets within the firm, thereby leading to new competencies. The outcome again is growth.

A Yellow growth strategy attends to the *long-term* growth of the organization. It is about sustainability. Whereas Blue and Red growth strategies focus on short-term results, Yellow keeps an eye on the long term. And the long term involves using the power of engagement, integration, and teamwork to create a growth strategy that draws its energy from *within* the organization.

For a company with a Yellow-focused strategy, investing in employees is a business necessity. The investment develops confidence in employees and builds team spirit. My favorite quote on the issue of team spirit is a poem that basketball coach Phil Jackson used to read to the Chicago Bulls before every playoff game:

> Now this is the Law of the Jungle –
> As old and as true as the sky;
> And the Wolf that shall keep it may prosper;
> But the Wolf that shall break it must die.
> As the creeper that girdles the tree trunk,
> The Law runneth forward and back –
> For the strength of the Pack is the Wolf,
> And the strength of the Wolf is the Pack.

– From Rudyard Kipling's *The Second Jungle Book* **quoted in** *Sacred Hoops: Spiritual Lessons of a Hardwood Warrior* **by Phil Jackson**

WHAT A STRONG YELLOW CULTURE DOES FOR ORGANIZATIONS

Organizations that have strong Yellow cultures have numerous advantages. Consider what happened in the U.S. airline industry after September 11, 2001. The terrorist attacks adversely affected the entire industry. Every airline downsized. Since the "short-haul" airlines were the most adversely affected—it's relatively easy for someone to drive from St. Louis to Kansas City rather than fly—these airlines felt the most pressure to downsize. Two major airlines in this category were Southwest and US Airways.

Figure 6.2 shows the downsizing each airline engaged in. Fast forward one year to late 2002. Every United States airline suffered a price decline over that year, as we would expect. However, the largest percentage price decline was suffered by US Airways. And the *smallest* percentage price decline was suffered by Southwest.

These data make a simple point. US Airways, a Blue company, acted in a manner consistent with its corporate culture. Southwest, with its celebrated Yellow culture, acted in a manner consistent with its corporate culture. The message Southwest sent to its employees was: "Look. Times are tough. Every airline is downsizing and laying people off. But

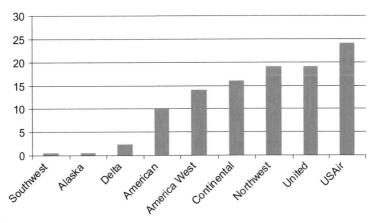

FIGURE 6.2

Downsizing of employment among U.S. airlines after 9/11/2001.

we will not do that. We will suffer short-term financial losses, but we will stand by you." What does this achieve?

It establishes an "implicit contract," as economists would say. The implicit contract is that the next time the going gets tough, Southwest may look to its employees to make personal sacrifices to help the company. A strong Yellow culture makes the organization more resilient. This makes it easier to implement riskier growth strategies.

Another example of the power of a strong Collaborate culture is the work done by Kaiser-Hill at the Rocky Flats Nuclear Arsenal, which is a site located 16 miles west of Denver.[5] A rocky but flat area at the foot of the Flatirons on the eastern slope of the Rockies, the site consists of a 385-acre industrial area surrounded by 6000 acres of open space buffer zone. Approximately 800 structures, or 3 million square feet under roof, existed at the site.

Beginning in 1951, the mission of this facility was radioactive and non-radioactive metal working and machining: plutonium recovery and research and development. The facility made the majority of nuclear weapons triggers—the nuclear component of missile warheads.

Thousands of highly skilled employees worked there. They had top-secret clearance and were very proud of their role in supporting national defense. A tight-knit culture existed. Productivity and efficiency were high.

Rocky Flats operated under the jurisdiction of the Atomic Energy Act. Because of security issues, no EPA monitoring was allowed. A shroud of secrecy surrounded the place. Numerous groups—environmentalists, citizen action groups, state regulatory agencies, federal oversight agencies, and even Congress—were consequently distrustful of Rocky Flats. Antagonism developed over time. The largest industrial fire in United States history occurred at the site in 1969. This and other accidents reinforced the view that this was a dangerous site.

Over time, things worsened. Workers handled almost every dangerous chemical produced in the United States. Yet safety was not carefully

---

[5] See Kim Cameron and Marc Lavine, *Making the Impossible Possible: Leading Extraordinary Performance: The Rocky Flats Story*, Berrett-Koehler Publishing, 2006. The book has an excellent account of this case and also a discussion of the importance of abundance and corporate culture.

monitored. And OSHA officials were barred from entering the site. The FBI ultimately raided the facility because of fears about pollution and environmental damage. President Bush closed the facility permanently in 1992. There was now a complete loss of mission.

But you don't just turn the switch off at a nuclear facility. The EPA came in with new requirements related to evidence of safety and non-pollution. Compliance requirements caused the workforce to balloon to 8000 from its previous level of 3500. But no work was done for six years. No advancement in soil decontamination, waste disposal, or building removal. No production could resume.

A number of contracting firms were hired to operate the site. Hundreds of unresolved grievances were filed. Antagonism, distrust, and low morale gripped the place. It cost $700 million per year just to keep the facility operating, for things such as security, water, air conditioning, and maintenance. The facility had to be closed for good. But that would cost a lot of money. The Department of Energy's estimate of closure and clean-up in 1995 was 70 years and $36 billion!

Into this situation stepped Kaiser-Hill. Leveraging its strong Collaborate culture and the power of abundance, it finished the job in 10 years. At a cost of $6 billion! And "the most dangerous place in America," according to ABC News' *Nightline*, was converted into a wildlife refuge—a huge and unexpected success.

TOOLS FOR DEVELOPING LEADERS

In its December 7, 2009, issue, *Fortune* published an article on the top 25 companies in the world for developing leaders.[6] There were 17 U.S. companies,[7] 3 Indian companies, 2 European companies, and 1 each in China, Singapore, and Brazil. So the question is: What do these companies do consistently better than others?

The following sections describe the three main things that strong Yellow organizations do especially well to develop their leadership pipelines.

---

[6] Beth Kowitt and Kim Thai, "The Top Companies for Leaders," *Fortune*, December 7, 2009, pp. 75–78.

[7] This includes McKinsey, for which the headquarters was listed as "none."

A Very Strong Corporate Culture

Each of these organizations has a very strong corporate culture that creates a sense of bonding and common values. Everybody in the organization knows the culture and the values embedded within it.[8] Everybody practices these values daily. And those who do not are not rewarded by promotions, even if they deliver outstanding results. Creating a common sense of purpose through a shared knowledge of culture requires effective communication. The use of the CVF as a tool of language can facilitate that.

Organizations Develop Employees as Leaders

Yellow organizations develop their employees as leaders by giving them "stretch assignments." These are assignments that take employees out of their comfort zones and ask them to do new things—achieve results in areas *outside* of their professional experiences or even educational training.

This can be achieved through exposing them to new *functional* challenges—asking someone with a marketing background to take on a finance challenge—or to new and unfamiliar geographies like posting an American in China or Ghana.[9] Jack Welch, when he was CEO of GE, was famous for doing this. He explained it as giving someone a shot and then seeing their confidence develop when they succeeded.

Commit to Employee Development

Strong Yellow organizations commit to employee development as a *long-term* strategy. They do not let short-term financial performance pressures sabotage the long-term employee development mission, even in recessions. Companies like Infosys in India and John Deere in the United States, both in the *Fortune* Top 25, are examples.

---

[8] For example, John Tolva, IBM's Chicago-based director of citizenship and technology, says, "What connects us is the values that IBM has instilled in us. It's a professional code that isn't written down but it's there." See Geoff Colvin, "How to Build Great Leaders," *Fortune*, December 7, 2009, pp. 70–72.

[9] For example, Colvin reports in his December 2009 *Fortune* article how John Deere sent an Indian-born U.S. citizen with a sales and marketing responsibility to China to learn more about the Chinese banking industry and how Deere could get working capital financing, even though he had no background in banking or China. Later, they put him in charge of logistics at a plant in Mexico. He had no background in logistics either.

LESSONS

There are three important lessons to take away from the discussions in this chapter.

- A strong Yellow culture can be developed by using the abundance concept. This means focusing on celebrating successes and coaxing the organization to achieve exemplary performance, rather than focusing on solving problems. Organizations with strong Yellow cultures are more resilient and more capable of absorbing the risks associated with aggressive growth strategies.

- Abundance requires a conscious effort to increase the ratio of positive to negative communication in the organization. In high-performance organizations, this ratio is between 3 and 9. Monitor the communication patterns in your organization and see how you come out.

- Strong Yellow companies develop their employees through stretch assignments, invest in employee development as a sustained long-term strategy, and have a strong culture that is commonly known and embraced throughout the organization.

I would like to end this chapter on a quote that exemplifies the potency of the positive and the essence of Yellow.

> Keep your thoughts positive, because your thoughts become your words. Keep your words positive, because your words become your behavior. Keep your behavior positive, because your behavior becomes your habits. Keep your habits positive because your habits become your values. Keep your values positive, because your values become your destiny.
> **– Mahatma Gandhi**

Reflection Exercise

As a leader in your organization, please choose a number from 1 to 5 to assign to each statement in Exercise 6.1.

Exercise 6.1

1 = Strongly disagree; 2 = Disagree; 3 = Neither agree nor disagree; 4 = Agree; 5 = Strongly agree

	1	2	3	4	5
(i) In our organization, there are more positive messages than negative messages.					
(ii) Our organization celebrates every meaningful success.					
(iii) Analyzing the reasons for negative variances and failures is more important in our organization than examining why we succeeded.					
(iv) People in our organization understand when we are performing at our very best.					
(v) People are the most important asset in our growth strategy.					
(vi) Financial capital is the most important asset in our growth strategy.					
(vii) Everybody in our organization can name our last major success.					
(viii) Everybody in our organization can explain the factors that accounted for our last major success.					
(ix) The ratio of positive to negative messages in our organization, on average, exceeds 3.					
(x) We develop our employees through "stretch assignments."					
(xi) We maintain our investment in the education and development of our employees even in the face of financial pressures.					

- Now ask various groups of employees to go through the same exercise.

- Then compare average responses across groups.

- What was learned as you reflected on your responses and those of other groups?

CHAPTER 7

Ideas for Red Growth Strategies

Let all things be done decently and in order.
– I Corinthians 14:40

Vasco Data Security International, Inc., is a company that sells digital encryption devices to banks to ensure the safety of financial information and foil would-be hackers. Located in Oakbrook Terrace, Illinois, the company had $88.8 million in sales and $16.4 million in earnings at the end of the March 31, 2007, fiscal year. Its story is an interesting example of a Red growth strategy.[1]

A man named T. Kendall Hunt became the CEO of the company in 1989. A start-up, Vasco had a contract to sell security devices to Dutch giant ABN AMRO Bank for its new dial-up banking option. The company was losing money when Hunt took over as CEO with an option to buy the company. Hunt proceeded to ruthlessly slash expenses. Headcount was cut from 30 to 4. By 1991, the company was profitable, and Hunt bought it. In 1998, it went public.

Hunt retired in 1999, but a softening of demand for Vasco's products led to financial challenges, so he came back in 2002. He once again cut the workforce and other expenses and slashed prices. The price reductions helped boost demand. Volume picked up. Scale economies kicked in. Combined with Vasco's technology lead over its competitors, the result was a 66% gross margin.

[1] See "Online Banking's Security Guard," *Business Week*, June 4, 2007.

A different story of the success of growth strategies supported by a Control-oriented focus is provided by many Indian companies.[2] In 2007, there was a spate of takeovers of foreign companies by Indian companies—a classic Blue growth strategy that was a striking demonstration of the confidence and global ambitions of these companies, and also an outcome of the fast-improving Red capabilities of these firms.

That year India's Tata Steel purchased the Dutch steel company Corus for $11.3 billion; wind turbine maker Suzlon Energy purchased German competitor REpower Systems for $530 million; and Sun Pharmaceuticals bid for an Israeli company, Taro Pharmaceutical Industries. Indian companies dominated the ranking of Asia's top 50 companies in 2007. And not just in information technology. Rather, the list included car manufacturers, mortgage lenders, and pharmaceutical companies.

What do these companies have in common apart from global ambitions? Smart management and low costs; in particular, these companies honed their Red cultures during a time when their very survival was at stake. For decades, India had a socialist economic system with central planning, closed markets, and ubiquitous interference by a multilayered government bureaucracy.
Companies were deprived of capital and technology, although government regulation kept foreign competitors out of the market too and protected domestic producers. Then came economic liberalization in the early 1990s. It gave Indian companies greater access to technology and capital. But it also opened the door for foreign competitors to enter.

Domestic competitors had to pick up their game. To compete effectively, Indian companies—those that survived—became super efficient. They

Photo from MSN

---

[2] See Manjeet Kripalani, "Indian Companies Hit Their Stride," *Business Week*, September 17, 2007.

cut costs, restructured, and upgraded their management talent. Adopting the best aspects of a Red culture was a matter of survival. But it also enabled these companies to acquire efficiency advantages that they would subsequently leverage through global acquisitions in order to grow.

An example of Red ingenuity by Indian companies is a recently publicized management practice called *jugaad*. It refers to improvisational innovation that is driven by scarce resources and the goal of meeting immediate customer needs. The idea is to cobble a product or service together in the least resource-intensive way and at the least cost.

Its proponents claim that *jugaad* has helped Indian companies, such as Tata Group and Infosys Technologies, gain a competitive advantage in a highly competitive marketplace and grow. Other companies, such as Best Buy, Cisco Systems, and Oracle, are already employing *jugaad* to create more economical products and services.[3]

WHAT GOOD RED COMPANIES DO TO GROW

The essence of a good Red organization can be described in one word: *execution*.

Execution, as a concept, is quite simple. It is simply the difference between what an individual, business unit, or company promises and what it delivers. This ability to execute and deliver results can provide the foundation for a cost and quality advantage in the marketplace. And if execution becomes an embedded part of the culture of the organization, then this can be a *sustainable* advantage.

What are the building blocks of execution? There are three:

- Leaders who understand execution
- A culture focused on execution
- The right people in the right place

---

[3] See Reena Jana, "India's Next Global Export: Innovation," *Business Week*, December 2, 2009. There are, however, detractors who claim that *jugaad* may also lead to cutting corners and compromising quality. Like so many things in life, the effectiveness of any tool depends on how it is used.

WHAT LEADERS NEED TO UNDERSTAND ABOUT EXECUTION

Execution is all about *process* and *ownership* of the agenda. Figure 7.1 shows the keys to creating the right process.

When it comes to prioritizing activities, the most important consideration is *strategic rationale*. This is followed by *doability*. Scoring easy wins early on is important. So the most doable tasks come first. Next comes *resource commitment*, followed by *time required*. Activities that require fewer resources and less time get done first.

After creating a timeline for the various activities, it is also important to break down each activity into many *small steps* and build in interim progress checks of these steps. Finally, after all the initially listed goals

FIGURE 7.1
Designing the right process.

are achieved, one should document all the areas where improvements are possible. It is imperative to engage the organization in continuous process improvement.

There are many companies where leaders not only understand execution but have developed organizational cultures that excel in execution. These cultures are built around centralized processes that generate efficiency. A good example is IBM. It has globally centralized key functions. Global procurement is centrally done from China. Global accounting is done from the Philippines.

A considerable amount of code writing is done in India. This allows IBM to establish a presence in a new geography with a relatively small organization, since the organization can rely on the centralized global IBM functions for its accounting, procurement, and so on.

A new $2 billion business can be established with as few as five or six people! This is because of uniform processes and very effective globalization. Whether it is human resources, marketing, acquisitions, or procurement, IBM has implemented a well-tried global process for it. The culture truly reflects the best of Red. A good process makes things easy for the organization. Execution becomes natural for people. Ambiguity is minimized. Reliability is maximized. This simple truth is as ancient as the *Rig Veda*, which was written more than 3000 years ago:

> I draw water from the fountain whose buckets are in place, with good straps, easy to draw water from, freely flowing and inexhaustible.
> **– *The Rig Veda*, as translated by Wendy Doniger O'Flaherty**

A company that exemplifies the power of process improvement is Dell, which was covered in Chapter 2. The company not only is an excellent Red, but has elevated the "document learning and improve process" part of process design to an art form. As a result, it has generated enough new business process ideas to gather hundreds of business-process patents.

Another good example is the brewing operation at Anheuser-Busch under Doug Muhleman (prior to when it was acquired by InBev). The relentless focus on quality resulted in consistently high-quality beer—good enough to help the company capture more than 50% market share in the United States.

WHAT IS A CULTURE FOCUSED ON EXECUTION?

When a culture is focused on execution, employees take *ownership* of the execution agenda. There are well-defined *metrics* to measure outcomes. There is *accountability*. There is *autonomy*. There are *rewards* for executing according to plan and for exceeding targets. And there are *punishments* for failing to do so.

Those in charge of execution are convinced of the importance and *power* of the execution agenda (see Figure 7.2). They are excited by it and they *own* it.

A good example of an execution-focused culture is Dell. It's a culture that helps the company zero in on problems as soon as they are

FIGURE 7.2
Representation of a culture focused on execution.

discovered. The problems are then dealt with quickly and directly. There is no room for excuses. Every dime is watched. Every product is expected to be profitable as soon as it is launched. Executives are expected to be in command of the facts—even the minutest details. Operating margin is a key metric every business is measured against. It is a culture that strives for constant improvement while attending to every small detail.

The results are impressive. Dell's revenue per employee is three times that of powerhouse IBM. And it is almost twice that of Hewlett-Packard.

Toyota is also legendary for its attention to process. In fact, it gained significant market share from its rivals worldwide and grew because of breakthrough improvements in process. Back in the 1960s, it took car manufacturers 6 to 8 hours to change the factory over from manufacturing one model to manufacturing another.

Then Toyota revolutionized the industry by introducing flexible manufacturing techniques and cut the model-changeover time to under a minute! Today every major car manufacturer does it in 40 seconds or so.

While Toyota has been the quality benchmark in the industry for decades, others have now caught up. J.D. Power has placed Buick (made by GM) and Jaguar ahead of Lexus and Toyota. Because Toyota's competitive edge in Red has been diminished, the battle is now being fought on the basis of the emotional appeal of automobiles to consumers.

Styling, cabin design, handling, and other such features now figure more prominently in the consumer's choice. Innovation, a Green activity, has become more important. Not an easy shift for an organization that excels in Red.

Partly as a result of this, competitors, such as BMW and Volkswagen, have recently out-competed Toyota. For example, while Toyota's sales fell 23.8% during 2009 in the U.S., Volkswagen experienced only a 6.6% decline.[4] The lesson is a familiar one. When the value driver shifts because of changes in the market, the strength that has sustained an organization that excels in one quadrant is no longer enough.

---

[4] See "Losing Its Shine," *The Economist*, December 12, 2009.

Toyota, however, also excels in Yellow. And that augurs well for it in the long run.

PUTTING THE RIGHT PEOPLE IN THE RIGHT PLACE

At the end of the day, one cannot execute with the wrong people (see Figure 7.3). Good Red leaders understand this all too well. Hiring, performance appraisal, and firing are all part and parcel of putting the right people in the right place.

Hiring the right people is a key organizational competency. The issue is not just one of technical competency. It is also a question of whether the individual's aptitude is compatible with the culture of the organization. This is critical.

Just as important as hiring is the *performance appraisal* that must occur on an ongoing basis after the individual is hired. Here is where companies with an execution-oriented culture truly differentiate themselves. In many organizations that lack a strong execution-oriented culture, there are far too many performance appraisals that tend to gloss over areas of underperformance and weakness. There is a reluctance to give bad appraisals. Candid feedback is important.

FIGURE 7.3
Executing with the right people.

This has two undesirable consequences. One is that employees do not receive the negative signals that can trigger efforts to improve. And the other is that when an underperforming employee is laid off during a downsizing, it is a complete shock to the employee. He has 30 years of good performance appraisals, so the firing seems inexplicable!

Firing low performers, especially when there is no companywide downsizing, is never easy for any executive. Too often the propensity is to procrastinate. Hope that the performance will improve when the economy gets better. But such procrastination can prove costly to the organization in terms of the opportunity cost of not bringing in a high performer to replace the underperformer. And worse still, it sends a signal to the rest of the organization that underperformance is tolerated. Just remember that everybody in the organization can evaluate everybody else.

Providing the right incentives to your winners—the high performers— is just as important. Perhaps even more important. One disease in some organizations is "corporate socialism." It is the practice of "smoothing out" rewards across individuals. One reason for doing this is to reduce the organizational costs that can arise because employees who receive lesser rewards envy those who receive more, and such envy can lead to counterproductive behavior.[5]

In performance-oriented organizations, this practice is minimized. There is no reluctance to celebrate the top performers, to reward them handsomely, and to let the others in the organization know the prizes that await them if they too perform at the highest level.

A good example of this is the compensation practice in investment banks. You make a profit for the bank and you get a bonus. The bigger the profit, the bigger the bonus. It is not unusual for a bond trader to make more than the CEO.[6]

---

[5] For a formal theoretical analysis, see Anand Goel and Anjan Thakor, "Green With Envy: Implications for Corporate Investment Distortions," *Journal of Business* 78 (6), 2005, pp. 2255–2287.
For an examination of the destructive behavior of envious agents, see Vai-Lam Mui, "The Economics of Envy," *Journal of Economic Behavior and Organization* 26, 1995, pp. 311–336.

[6] Some might view the recent implosion of the investment banking industry as an indictment of this practice. But that is like throwing out the baby with the bathwater. Positive compensation incentives can motivate employees to work harder, but they cannot eliminate hubris.

Apart from its obvious incentive effect for the rest of the organization, the practice of handsomely rewarding your top performers has another benefit. It helps to retain your top talent. Jack Welch tells the story of how he almost quit GE early in his career because he was given the same raise as everybody else.

PERFORMANCE METRICS AND ALIGNMENT

Another attribute of good Red organizations is that they make effective use of performance metrics. There are three conditions that performance metrics in good Red organizations satisfy:

Metrics Are Linked to Value Creation

Often performance metrics based on accounting measures—like net income—can distort behavior and possibly even lead to value destruction. Consider the case of a major pharmaceutical company that decided to reward managers based on net income growth and found that R&D investments—classified as expenses on the income statement—were slashed. This boosted net income, but it also sacrificed the pipeline of new drugs that is the lifeblood of a pharmaceutical company.

By contrast, good Red companies adopt performance metrics that are linked to *economic value creation.* For example, when SPX adopted Economic Value Added (EVA) in 1996, employees responded by uncovering hundreds of ways to create value. The stock price jumped from $40.375 in December 1996 to above $78 by the first quarter of 1998.

Metrics Are Linked to the Growth Strategy

Organizations that make effective use of performance metrics deliberately design them to influence employee behavior so that it is *aligned* with the company's growth strategy. For example, Enterprise Rent-A-Car's growth strategy is significantly dependent on customer satisfaction. To align employee behavior with customer satisfaction, promotions of employees in any given location are linked to whether customer satisfaction exceeds a target level.

Performance Metrics Are Not Plentiful

Generally, everybody understands how projects, people, and business units are being judged. Effective use of performance metrics requires that employees understand *how* these metrics will be used, and how what they do will affect how people will be judged with those metrics. Without this clarity, metrics are not terribly useful.

In addition, one thing that such clarity requires is that there is not a plethora of metrics to confuse people. The more metrics you have, the less clear it is how important each metric is and the more likely it is that the metrics may pull employees in different directions. Focus and alignment are replaced by confusion. The good Red organizations use a few metrics and clarify to their employees how their actions can affect these metrics.

Properly deployed, performance metrics can be an effective tool for organizational alignment. They can help focus and align employee behavior with the organization's growth strategy.

Figure 7.4 provides a summary of what the best-in-class control-oriented (Red) companies do.

LESSONS

The following key takeaways have emerged from our discussions in this chapter.

- A company with a growth strategy that is based on Control focuses on execution.

- The three building blocks of execution are: leaders who understand execution, a culture focused on execution, and the right people in the right place.

- Organizations that focus on Control also make effective use of performance metrics to achieve alignment.

FIGURE 7.4
Best practices of Red organizations.

- Companies that develop execution-focused cultures develop a sustainable competitive advantage over their rivals and are also able to globalize more effectively.

The techniques of efficiency (e.g., Six-Sigma or Lean-Sigma) will always be copied by your competitors. What is much more difficult to copy is an execution-focused Red culture. It is the strength of such a culture that can provide the competitive advantage that translates into sustained growth.

Reflection Exercise

As a leader in your organization, please choose a number from 1 to 5 to assign to each statement in Exercise 7.1.

Exercise 7.1

1 = Strongly disagree; 2 = Disagree; 3 = Neither agree nor disagree; 4 = Agree; 5 = Strongly agree

	1	2	3	4	5
(i) Our organization has clearly defined goals that are easily understood by all.					
(ii) We have a well-articulated strategy for execution to achieve these goals.					
(iii) We have clear metrics for measuring progress in the various activities needed to execute our strategy.					
(iv) We conduct interim progress checks and take appropriate corrective action.					
(v) We routinely document what we learn during execution of our initiatives and constantly improve our processes.					
(vi) Our employees have considerable autonomy in achieving their targets.					
(vii) There is a high degree of accountability in our organization.					
(viii) We provide candid performance appraisals.					
(ix) Underperformers in our organization are eventually let go.					
(x) Top performers are handsomely rewarded in our organization.					
(xi) We (managers) have a small number of value-based performance metrics that are linked to our growth strategy and are clearly understood by all.					

- Have different groups in the organization go through this exercise.

- Discuss the average scores across groups.

- What action steps does this exercise help your organization to come up with?

CHAPTER 8

Ideas for Blue Growth Strategies

> Now let's suit up. And let's murmur a prayer for any opponents that dare get in our way. They're going to need all the help they can get.
> — Lou Holtz in *Winning Every Day*

During the 1990s, Cisco acquired as many as 75 companies a year to grow. Most of these companies had new technologies that Cisco wanted access to. Many were relatively small companies and easy to integrate.

NationsBank (prior to its merger with Bank of America, which then created a larger bank with that name) built a national banking franchise through strategic acquisitions. The acquisition of many different banks allowed NationsBank to identify opportunities that existed in the white spaces between the products they were offering prior to acquisition.

While companies like Cisco and NationsBank/Bank of America have used acquisitions as a Blue growth strategy, other companies have used special events to launch new products that expand their reach in existing markets. The 2008 Beijing Olympics proved to be a profitable special event for many companies in this regard.

One area in which companies found opportunities was security. The goal of keeping the Olympics secure was very important to the Chinese government. So it spent about $6 billion on security. *Many companies' Blue growth strategies were facilitated by this.* For example,

95

Photo from *Business Week*

FIGURE 8.1
Photograph of some of Segway's electric-power scooters.

Segway, which makes two-wheeled electric-powered scooters at $5300 each, sold more than 100 of these for use by police and other personnel from security agencies (see Figure 8.1).[1]

GE was significantly involved in providing security for the Olympics. It supplied detection systems at the Beijing airport to sniff out particles in the air related to bombs or drugs. It installed video surveillance devices on subways and in buildings. And it won the entire security contract for the new headquarters of the Chinese national broadcaster CCTV.

The payoff for these companies is not just the revenue generated from these Olympics-related sales. It goes far beyond that. It's an important step in breaking into (pardon the pun) the Chinese security market. A market worth about $11 billion and expected to grow!

What we have discussed are but a few examples of Blue growth strategies. In this chapter, we will see what the best-in-class Blue companies do to grow. The essence of a good Blue strategy lies in two key elements: speed and market focus.

GROWTH STRATEGIES OF BLUE COMPANIES

Figure 8.2 provides a systematic categorization of Blue growth strategies. The five growth strategies shown there should not be viewed as being mutually exclusive, however. Companies often use different growth strategies—even if they are all Blue—in different stages of the

---

[1] See Dexter Roberts, "Olympics Security Is No Game," *Business Week*, August 18, 2008.

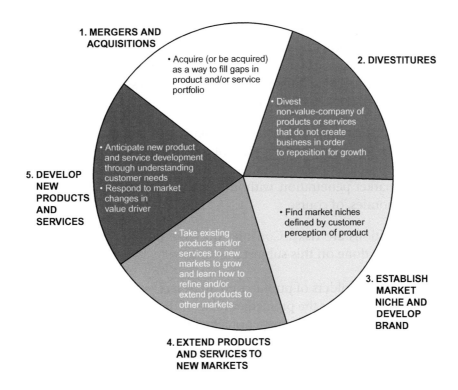

FIGURE 8.2
Blue growth strategies.

product life cycle. The key is to understand that all these strategies are available. And to know when it is optimal to employ a specific growth strategy.

Mergers and Acquisitions

Numerous companies have used mergers and acquisitions (M&A) as a successful growth strategy. For example, Smith & Wesson Holding Corp., a gun maker that represents one of the most recognizable brands in the world, acquired Thompson/Center Arms, a leading manufacturer of rifles. The kinds of guns Thompson makes represent an annual $1.1 billion market. Moreover, Thompson's manufacturing expertise with longer barrels also gives Smith & Wesson the capability to develop products that will facilitate penetration in other markets.

Mergers and acquisitions is also a useful strategy in highly fragmented markets. Acquisitions in such markets are called "roll-ups." They help eliminate duplication and asset redundancies, and take advantage of scale economies. Blockbuster used roll-ups successfully in the video market to establish a national presence.

After the dismantling of interstate banking restrictions in the United States in 1994, we witnessed a wave of roll-ups in banking. Large banks gobbled up smaller regional and local banks. In most cases, the rationale was market penetration without creating asset redundancies—and scale economies, of course.

But acquisitions are risky. Consider the nine findings from the scientific research done on this subject that follow:

1. Target shareholders of public companies receive an average premium of 20 to 30% over the premerger value of their shares, depending on whether it is a friendly merger or a hostile tender offer.

2. On average, the shareholders of acquiring firms do not gain in acquisitions. The average "abnormal" return (that is their return after removing the effects of movements in the overall stock market) for the acquirer upon the announcement of the acquisition is −0.5% to −0.7%.

3. Acquiring firms also report significantly negative abnormal returns over a multiyear period after the consummation of the transaction. (See Figure 8.3.)

The figure shows what statisticians call a histogram. The x-axis represents the abnormal or "excess" shareholder returns earned by acquirers during a period starting 10 days prior to the announcement of the acquisition to 1 or 2 years later. The excess return is that left over after controlling for market movements.

The y-axis represents the percentage of firms in the sample that experienced those returns. So, for example, about 23% of all acquirers earned excess returns of *less than or equal to* −40% (i.e., −40% or worse) during the time period starting 10 days prior to the acquisition announcement and ending 2 years after the announcement.

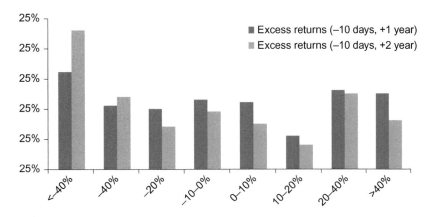

FIGURE 8.3

Distribution of long-term excess returns for acquirers.

Source: Citigroup and Hazelkorn, Zenner, and Shivdasani, "Creating Value with Mergers and Acquisitions," *Journal of Applied Corporate Finance*, Spring/Summer, 2004.

Figure 8.3 reveals a couple of interesting patterns:

- This is *not* the usual bell-shaped curve. The majority of observations are *not* in the middle (represented by 0% excess return).

- The distribution of returns has "fat tails." That means it has plenty of observations at the extremes—lots of big winners and big losers. Focusing on the (-10 days, $+2$ years) time period, about 20% of the acquirers earned abnormal returns of 20% or more. But about 35% of acquirers earned returns of -20% or worse!

Now let's return to what researchers have found out about the risks of acquisitions.

4. Diversification-causing mergers result in value losses on average for acquirers.

5. Acquisitions of more mature targets are on average *better received* by the stock market than acquisitions of targets with high expected earnings growth.

6. Although acquirers often overestimate both revenue and cost synergies, revenue synergies are overestimated more frequently than are cost synergies.

7. Controlling for the size of the acquisition and the terms of payment, the stock market reacts *more positively* to acquisitions of private companies, or units or assets of public companies, than to acquisitions of whole public companies.

8. During the 1991–2001 time period, based on the stock returns of acquirers over the 3 days following the announcement, U.S. acquiring firms' shareholders lost $217 billion in shareholder wealth.[2]

So what do we take away from the preceding research findings?

On average, firms do not create value for their shareholders via acquisitions. And diversification-causing acquisitions do worse than others. The amount of wealth of shareholders in acquiring firms that is destroyed through acquisitions is enormous. But if an acquirer you must be, then acquiring more mature targets and private companies or units of public companies represents your best strategy.

Mature targets are better than high-growth targets because it's likely that hefty premiums will be paid for (often unproven) growth prospects. And avoiding acquisitions of whole public companies helps because a 20 to 30% premium over the preacquisition stock price of the target can be avoided.[3]

Does this mean one should not acquire? Most emphatically not. It just suggests caution. Moreover, remember from Figure 8.3 that there are some companies that are big winners in acquisitions. In fact, the final scientific evidence point about risky acquisitions says:

9. Targets and acquirers *combined* experience a value gain from acquisitions.

---

[2] See Sara Moeller, Frederick Schlingemann, and René Stulz, "Wealth Destruction on a Massive Scale? A Study of Acquiring Firm Returns in the Recent Merger Wave," *Journal of Finance* 60 (2), 2005, pp. 757–782.

[3] Part of the reason for this is that with acquisitions of whole public companies, there is a "reference point" effect. The target's stock price serves as a reference point for the acquisition price. See Malcolm Baker and Jeffrey Wurgler, "A Reference Point Theory of Mergers and Acquisitions," paper presented at the American Financial Association Meeting, January 2010. Such a reference point does not exist for acquisitions of divisions or private companies.

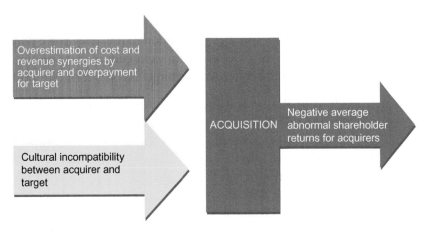

FIGURE 8.4

Why acquisitions don't produce wealth for acquirers on average.

So mergers and acquisitions do create total value. And they are particularly valuable in cases in which the firm can use them to fill gaps in its product portfolio. But acquirers lose on average. Target shareholders gain. This suggests that at least part of the problem is the *division* of gains from the merger between the acquirer and the target. In fact, Figure 8.4 indicates the main reasons why mergers don't work well for acquirers on average.

We have already discussed the issue of overestimating synergies and paying too much for a target as a consequence. Quite often, the overpayment comes about due to a lack of financial discipline in the valuation. This is a Red (process) failure. Other times it results from "deal momentum"—"I know the CEO wants this deal to go through for strategic reasons, so why should I step in front of a speeding train?" In this regard, there are two truths worth remembering:

- Don't do the deal if it does *not* fit your growth strategy.

- Don't do the deal for strategic reasons if the price is too high.

In fact, as Harry Tempest, former CEO of ABN AMRO North America, once said:

> We have a rule on the Executive committee. When someone says "strategic," the rest of us say "too expensive."

The issue of corporate culture is even tougher to deal with. It's a yellow problem. It's very important, but too often ignored. It is easy to see why. If we do not have a clear diagnosis of even our own culture, how can we go about examining whether the culture of the target is compatible with ours?

A research study into the importance of culture has uncovered striking results.[4] It examined 106 mergers over a 10-year time period. The researchers had the CVF culture profiles of the acquirers and the targets, so they could assess whether the cultures of the merging firms were compatible. They then classified successful mergers as those in which acquirers earned +20% abnormal returns—over and above the returns required to compensate shareholders for risk—and unsuccessful mergers as those in which acquirers earned −20% or worse.

What the study found is that a measure of organizational culture is highly correlated (96%) with successful and unsuccessful mergers. That is, this study suggests that culture is particularly important in the "tails"—for the highly successful and the highly unsuccessful mergers.

So, what do the successful acquirers do that we can learn from? Based on a study by McKinsey as well as other research, Figure 8.5 provides a summary. Note once again the importance of *alignment*.

Divestitures

Although it seems odd to talk about divestitures in a discussion of growth strategies, sometimes it is better to shrink now in order to grow later, for two reasons. One is that the divestiture of value-destroying business units can increase the firm's equity market value right away. The research evidence shows:

10. Refocusing divestitures increases the equity market value of the divesting firm and also improves its operating performance.

The other reason why divestitures often help is that they allow the resources of the organization to be focused on what it does best. It liberates it to focus on areas where abundance can be practiced. A great example of this is provided in the following case of General Dynamics.

---

[4] Kim Cameron and Carlos Mora, "Corporate Culture and Financial Success of Mergers and Acquisitions," working paper, The University of Michigan, 2003.

1. M&A is viewed as a tool to fill strategic holes (e.g., diversifying an asset profile or expanding geographic footprint) rather than a growth strategy.
2. Postacquisition strategy for target is mapped out in detail prior to the acquisition.
3. High degree of autonomy for target managers along with high accountability.
4. Generally, 80% of acquirers retained senior target executives after acquisition.
5. Postacquisition integration completed in less than one year, suggesting that successful acquirers take cultural compatibility into account.
6. Compensation is highly performance sensitive (bonuses up to 80–100% of base pay) and tied to both short-term (e.g., working capital management) and long-term (e.g., RONA, EVA) drivers of value.
7. Business units are involved from start to finish—origination, due diligence, negotiation, and integration—especially in "bolt-on" acquisitions (i.e., those similar to acquirer's existing operations).
8. Postacquisition integration teams include members of due-diligence team.
9. Great deal of attention is focused on who is appointed to the top management team and how people who exit are treated.
10. *Alignment* of the top team is a top priority.

FIGURE 8.5
Best practices of successful acquirers from research evidence.

GENERAL DYNAMICS CASE STUDY

In 1991, defense contractor General Dynamics engaged a new management team and instructed it to maximize shareholder value; the following text is from the author's work there.[5] At that time the defense contracting industry in general was faced with declining demand and excess capacity projections.

Many firms responded by making defense-related acquisitions and diversifying into nondefense businesses. But General Dynamics chose to focus on shareholder value and undertook many painful initiatives in anticipation of forthcoming problems instead of waiting until the problems were at the company's doorstep. How General Dynamics managed to do this illustrates the way a company can excel in the Compete quadrant.

Lockheed Martin F-16 Fighting Falcon developed by General Dynamics.

From *www.livingwarbirds.com*

---

[5] Adapted from Anjan Thakor, *Becoming a Better Value Creator*. San Francisco: Jossey-Bass, 2000.

The origins of General Dynamics can be traced back to 1899, when it began as the Electric Boat Company. It became a major supplier of submarines and cargo ships to the U.S. Navy during both World Wars. By 1960, it was a major manufacturer of aircraft, booster rockets, and missiles, and it dominated the nuclear submarine business. It was around this time that it was renamed General Dynamics.

Over the next three decades the company grew impressively, fueled in part by its foreign sales. Its products included the F16 jet fighter, the M-1 and M-60 Abrams tanks, and eventually civilian aircraft (a capability it acquired as a result of purchasing Cessna).

On September 27, 1989, the company announced the hiring of William Anders as CEO. Anders was a former U.S. Air Force pilot and Apollo 8 astronaut who had orbited the moon during Christmas 1968. At the time the appointment was announced, defense contracting was a growth industry. Anders was scheduled to become CEO on January 1, 1991.

Between the announcement of his appointment and actually taking over as CEO, Anders saw the outlook for the industry change dramatically. The Soviet Union disintegrated in 1990 and the Berlin Wall fell the same year, signaling the end of the Cold War. By the time Anders took the helm, the forecast of a reduced demand for General Dynamics' products was as plain as the proverbial writing on the wall.

As soon as he stepped up to the plate, Anders made it very clear that his goal was to transform General Dynamics into a shareholder-value-driven enterprise. He articulated three financial goals:

- Increase return on assets
- Improve product profit margin
- Focus more sharply on investments

What followed was as fundamental a transformation of an organization as almost any in recent corporate history.

Anders' constructive assault on General Dynamics was two-pronged. One prong involved putting in place an organizational change plan that involved changing mindsets, incentives, knowledge, and behavior. The other prong involved implementing a shareholder-value-focused strategy for the company.

The organizational change plan had five principal elements. First, a new management team was appointed. Eighteen of the top 25 executives were either new to General Dynamics or new to their positions. Second, Anders invited a Wall Street analyst to alert top management and directors to the severity of the company's situation. The analyst noted that the company's Price/Earnings (P/E) ratio ranked 497th in the S&P 500. A sobering reminder of the stock market's assessment of the company's future growth potential.

Third, Anders promoted James Mellor, who had been executive vice president in charge of submarines, tanks, and overseas sales, to president and chief operating officer. Anders described Mellor's role as follows:

> We talked a lot about focusing on shareholder value and each of our top executives was committed to this objective. Even though that was our *focus*, it was not our *strategy* because maximizing shareholder value is difficult to operationalize. Mellor really helped the managers

understand how to run their businesses. Just accepting the idea of shareholder value isn't enough. For a lot of the managers, it was a case of "OK, I believe in shareholder value, but what should I do tomorrow?" Mellor taught them how to manage for cash.

Fourth, the company was divided into business areas, and decision-making authority was pushed further down into the hierarchy. To help managers adjust to their newly expanded roles, Mellor asked a top business school to develop a special one-week seminar for 150 of the company's managers. The seminar covered business basics and investment analysis so that General Dynamics' managers would "think like business people, not aerospace engineers."

Fifth, to focus his management team on maximizing shareholder value, Anders reengineered the company's executive compensation system. All links to accounting measures of performance were eliminated. Compensation was tied to the General Dynamics stock price through stock options, and incentives were provided for employees to hold onto their stock positions.

Under the plan, 25 top executives would receive approximately 1.5% of the increase in shareholder value for the first $10 increase in stock price and 3% for subsequent 10% increases in stock price. And unlike many incentive compensation plans, the plan did not impose any limit on the amount of bonuses as long as the stock price continued to increase.

The new management compensation plan was not without its detractors. The company's unionized workforce was openly critical. Many were outraged that senior executives could earn large bonuses while the rank and file were being laid off. Compensation consultant Graef Crystal voiced his criticism as follows: "This is a case of a guy getting lots of money, and he's an island of prosperity in a sea of misery." Crystal also said, "The CEO of General Dynamics must be the laziest man in the world. Look at all the incentive plans they have to give him to go to work in the morning."

The emotion behind such criticism is understandable. But it has little economic merit. To Anders' credit, he persisted despite the criticism. Anders also defined a new strategy for the company. His strategy had the following three elements.

First, the company would eschew diversification into nondefense businesses. In line with this, General Dynamics announced in October 1997 that its largest nondefense subsidiary, Cessna Aircraft, was for sale. Moreover, the company said it would study all of its nondefense operations as possible divestiture candidates.

Second, Anders provided industry leadership by publicly urging the industry to both downsize and consolidate. His mantra was: "No one should invest and grow in the defense industry."

Third, like General Electric, General Dynamics announced that it would remain only in businesses where it could both be #1 or #2 and achieve a "critical mass" to justify dedicated factories. Anders identified four businesses within the company's "core capabilities" that passed these two tests: military aircraft, nuclear submarines, tanks, and space systems. He then announced a formal plan of contraction in which the company would seek to sell units outside these four areas.

As a consequence of implementing this strategy, General Dynamics' sales decreased 66% from $9.5 billion in 1991 to $3.2 billion in 1993. Anders remarked, "Although human and physical assets would ultimately have to leave the industry, GD's assets were in general being consolidated into other companies."

Even before the results of the company's organizational change plan and strategy were known, three Wall Street firms put General Dynamics on their "buy list." Why? Because of the new incentive plan focusing on shareholder wealth, the reduced capital and R&D spending, and the possibility of stock repurchases to return cash to shareholders.

By the time Anders had been in his job as CEO for about three years, spectacular shareholder value had been created. Every $100 invested in General Dynamics in January 1991, when Anders came on board, was worth $653 by December 1993, including cash dividends and reinvestments. Over this time, the value-weighted defense industry portfolio (excluding General Dynamics) was worth $214 per original $100 and the S&P 500 was worth $155.

The market value of General Dynamics' equity was $1 billion in January 1991. By December 1993, it was $4.5 billion. The company had shrunk to a third of its size in terms of sales and had grown four and a half times in terms of the market value of its equity. Somewhere between $2.3 billion and $3.5 billion of the company's market value of equity was directly attributable to management actions under Anders.

General Dynamics grew subsequently. By year-end 2007, it had annual sales of $27.24 billion. By December 2008, it had a market value of equity of $22.34 billion.

Establish a Market Niche and Develop a Brand

Apart from M&A and repositioning from growth through divestitures, a company can also find an unoccupied market niche and then develop its brand in that niche—like Starbucks did.

In 1987, P&G (Folgers), General Foods (with Maxwell House), and Nestlé (with Nescafé) held 90% of the $8 billion retail coffee market (see Figure 8.6). But margins for all the players were vanishing. Health concerns had caused coffee consumption to fall to 1.67 cups/day per capita. That was down from a high of 3.1 cups/day in 1962.

The fundamental assumption that the industry was operating under was that coffee was a commodity for which consumers would never pay a premium. The majors all mass-produced ground coffee that was vacuum-packed for long shelf life. Their customer base was the entire grocery-buying public. Perhaps the biggest impediment to creating value was the consumer's perception of coffee.

From *www.creativemag.com*

FIGURE 8.6
Generic grocery store coffee display.

Into this industry stepped Howard Schultz with his now-famous concept of high-quality coffee served in cafés located close to places of work. And the initial customer base was upwardly mobile professionals. The first Starbucks café was introduced in Seattle in April 1986. Within a year, there were three cafés. By 1991, sales of $800 million, a market share of sales revenue of 17.7%, and a share of *market value* of 30%!

Starbucks and others like it had found a previously untapped market niche—a white space of sorts. These players used expensive Arabica beans, which were more aromatic and flavorful than the Robusta beans used by the major coffee makers. The coffee was fresher, higher quality, and available on-the-go as you went to work. It was priced 80% to 100% higher than traditional coffee. The rest, as they say, is history.

Another example of a company with a niche Blue growth strategy is Liquidity Services, Inc., located in Washington, D.C.[6] It has positioned itself for growth in the online marketplace for resale of surplus inventory. The company helps organizations auction off anything they wish to get off their books—cavalry horses, iPods, military surplus, finished goods, and so on. The company has 600,000 registered buyers for its auctions. It makes money by taking a commission on the items it sells—not by charging listing fees like some other auction sites.

---

[6] See Lorraine Woellert, "Sell It Again, Sam," *Business Week*, June 4, 2007.

Its 2007 sales were $173 million. Earnings were $9.4 million. The company is changing the game in the highly fragmented liquidation industry and is poised for high growth in the future.

Many retailers in the industry rely on local buyers who pay cash and take away the goods being sold at short notice. By contrast, Liquidity Services determines the ideal lot size for a product, gathers would-be buyers, manages the bidding, and handles the final financial transaction. Its niche is that its business design brings significant scale economies. These scale economies distinguish Liquidity Services from its competitors.

Extend Products and Services to New Markets

Sometimes companies get opportunities to take their products and services to new markets—new geographies and new customers. Being in unfamiliar territory can be risky and uncomfortable for the companies involved, especially because it may require the products or services to be adapted to the new market conditions. But the benefit is that it may allow the company to develop new competencies and possibly new products and services that can be brought back to the company's more established markets.

An example of this is Philadelphia food giant ARAMARK. The company has had considerable experience in providing food services at the Olympics, having catered to 13 Olympics since 1968.[7] However, serving food at the Beijing Olympics in 2008 provided the company with its biggest challenge yet.

The challenge had many dimensions: the very large scale of the project (serving 10,000 people per hour), the underdeveloped food distribution system in China, the difficulty of finding Western-style food products like cheese, convincing the athletes about the safety of the food being served in light of China's reputation for using high levels of pesticides and hormones in food production, and teaching servers to make eye contact with customers ordering food.

---

[7] See Nanette Byrnes, "3.5 Million Meals in 16 Days," *Business Week*, August 18, 2008.

What benefits did ARAMARK derive from this besides the profits from its Olympics contract? First, the company learned a lot about managing complex logistics in foreign markets—lessons that will prove useful in other markets. Moreover, as we saw in Chapter 6, this is also a Yellow tool for developing leaders. Second, it gave ARAMARK useful exposure to the Chinese market for obtaining more business from other companies. It already runs employee cafeterias for Dell, Lenovo Group, and Toyota.

Another example is the retailer Lotte, which is South Korea's biggest department store chain, with $5.8 billion in sales. Its strategy is to serve the new rich in emerging markets.[8] It entered Russia in 2007, but has had a hard time. Problems have included the amount it has had to spend on advertising to develop its brand. Attracting experienced staff locally has also proven to be difficult. Consequently, the company has been forced to lower its sales target in Russia.

From *www.visitkorea.or.kr*

But this has not deterred Lotte from trying elsewhere. In 2008, it entered China, setting up shop in Beijing. It has plans to open nine more stores in various Chinese cities.

Penetrating the Chinese market will not necessarily be easy for Lotte. Its market niche appears to be an extraordinarily courteous and

---

[8] See "Lotte Ambition: A South Korean Retailer Plans a Bold Move into China," *The Economist*, June 28, 2008.

friendly staff selling an attractive combination of local and foreign brands. With fewer cultural differences in China relative to its domestic Korean market than those it encountered in Russia, the company is optimistic about its prospects. The leadership development opportunities this will provide for Lotte's managers will also be invaluable.

Develop New Products and Services

A Blue growth strategy that creates new products and services comes about as a result of company-solicited customer feedback that reveals unmet customer needs and suggests new features that can be added to an existing product or service.

An example will illustrate the concept. EMC^2 is a highly successful company in the computer industry. It makes data storage equipment.[9] Under former CEO Michael Ruettgers, the company achieved a 35% market share in industrial-strength storage systems. From March 1998 to March 1999, EMC^2 shareholders earned an impressive return of 167%. That was a better performance than the shareholder returns delivered that year by the likes of Microsoft, Intel, Cisco, and Dell.

One of the keys to EMC's success during those years was its approach to product innovation. It adopted a policy of deliberately cannibalizing products at the peak of their sales cycle—20% per year for the next two years—by introducing the next generation of products. The idea was to stay in close touch with customers and discover what it was that they did not like about EMC's product, to learn from this feedback, and use it to develop the next generation of the product.

For example, while he was talking to a John Deere data center manager, Ruettgers learned that the computer networks' new servers

---

[9] See Anjan V. Thakor, *"Becoming a Better Value Creator,"* Jossey-Bass, pp. 152–154, 2000.

crashed more often than the mainframes. As a result, there was a lot of important information that was now scattered across many different machines that did not "talk to each other."

Ruettgers' insight was in visualizing a single storage system that could hold data from many other computers. The problem in introducing this new product was that it would cannibalize a successful existing product. Nonetheless, the company decided to go ahead with the new product—Symmetrix "open storage" systems.

My second example is less conventional. Cricket is as popular a sport in the United Kingdom and countries in the former British Commonwealth as baseball is in the United States. For a very long time, countries competed against each other in "test matches" (see Figure 8.7).

A test match used to last five days. Shockingly long by the standards of any other sport, but something that cricket fans were used to. Over time, however, shorter versions of these matches emerged, most notably one-day cricket matches. This was in response to perceived market demand for a game that took less time.

From *www.thegoogly.com*

FIGURE 8.7
Cricket is very popular in former British Commonwealth countries.

But the development that shook the world of cricket to its very foundations was the formation of the Indian Premier League (IPL) by a man named Lalit Modi.[10] The IPL is an eight-team league in which the teams are owned mostly by Indian industrialists and film stars. Players from all over the world are recruited to play. The format is the shortest ever in cricket—a game takes only three hours. Moreover, the focus is on entertainment. With cheerleaders and the like, the setup is more like an NFL football game than a cricket match.

The major source of revenue is expected to be from television, and the first-year championship game had a TV viewership of 36 million people. The league not only is off to a good start, but is also forcing countries around the world to consider scheduling their cricket matches during a time that does not conflict with the IPL schedule.

The very short time to finish a cricket game and the deft combination of the sport with entertainment through the formation of a league with eight teams was a major innovation in cricket. It came about because of an astute understanding of customer needs and the willingness to innovate.

Blue new product development, particularly of those that deliberately cannibalize your own products, has two big advantages over the conventional approach of replacing an existing product with a new product only when the existing product is in decline.

First, it keeps the organization always close to the customer and focused on constant improvement. That is energizing. Second, replacing a product at the peak of its sales cycle with an even better product makes it very difficult for competitors to copy you. Just when they are ready to bring to market a product that competes with your successful product, you have moved on. To an even better product. It can drive your competitors crazy.

RESPOND TO MARKET CHANGES IN YOUR VALUE DRIVER

Another source of Blue product innovation is the change in the key value driver of your growth strategy that may be caused by shifts in

---

[10] See "Cricket, Lovely Cricket," *The Economist*, August 2, 2008.

market demand conditions. These shifts may be due to changes in consumer preferences or new technologies. Time and again, highly successful companies have been caught off guard by such shifts.

We discussed in Chapter 7 how Toyota began to lose its competitive edge when its product quality no longer provided a sufficient competitive advantage and emotional appeal to consumers became a bigger competitive differentiator. Dell has faced a similar challenge. Its fast-delivery, low-cost model has been assaulted by a shift in consumer preferences for PCs that also have styling and emotional appeal.

As we saw in Chapter 4, Wal-Mart is coping with a major competitive challenge from Target, which is exploiting a shift in its own value driver. Starbucks is another example. It is recognizing that its expansion may have been too aggressive. There is a shift in consumer preferences that suggests that the value driver that anchors its strategy has changed somewhat—demand is not as high as anticipated.

When your value driver shifts, your growth strategy needs to adapt. This may require changes in your products and services. Sometimes fundamental changes. But these changes are also opportunities to re-energize the organization and reposition it for growth. Such repositioning will call for *realigning* the organization with the new growth strategy. The key is to have someone in the organization constantly assessing whether the value driver has changed.

LESSONS

Blue growth strategies are distinct. The lessons from this chapter are as follows.

- There are five types of Blue growth strategies:
  - Mergers and acquisitions
  - Using divestitures to reposition for growth
  - Establishing a market niche and developing a brand
  - Extending products and services to new markets
  - Blue new product development, including that necessitated by shifts in the company's value driver

- Acquisitions can be a very useful part of a Blue growth strategy. However, on average acquirers do not create value for their shareholders. This is despite the fact that the total gains from mergers, on average, are positive.

- The main reasons for the failure of acquirers to create value are overpayment and not taking into account cultural incompatibility between the acquirer and the target.

- Finding a market niche is all about discovering a customer need not being currently satisfied by the existing players.

- Extending existing products and services to new markets not only provides additional revenue sources but also helps the firm to learn. This learning can enhance revenues down the road. Moreover, it can provide "stretch assignments" for managers to develop their leadership capabilities.

- Blue new product development, based on customer feedback that provides information about unmet customer needs or shifts in the firm's value driver, allows firms to develop new products that are extension/refinements of existing products. These new products may cannibalize existing products—and deliberately too. This can provide a significant advantage over competitors.

Regardless of which kind of Blue growth strategy one is pursuing, the essential elements of any Blue strategy are speed and a market (including customer) focus. These are the elements that distinguish Blue.

Reflection Exercise

As a leader in your organization, please choose a number from 1 to 5 to assign to each statement in Exercise 8.1. After completing the exercise, doing the following is suggested:

- Compute the average score over the average scores on all six questions. The higher the score, the more Blue is your growth strategy.

- Based on this exercise, how Blue is your organization's growth strategy?

- Engage various groups within the organization in this discussion.

Exercise 8.1

1 = Strongly disagree; 2 = Disagree; 3 = Neither agree nor disagree; 4 = Agree; 5 = Strongly agree

	1	2	3	4	5
(i) The majority of our acquisitions have produced returns for our shareholders exceeding the cost of capital.					
(ii) We pay careful attention to corporate culture when determining whether to acquire a company.					
(iii) Our organization would be willing to divest unproductive assets and shrink in size in order to reposition for growth.					
(iv) We pay close attention to the spaces adjacent to existing products and services in the market to discover new niches.					
(v) We often make decisions to enter new markets and geographic areas with our products.					
(vi) We are happy to cannibalize our existing products in order to introduce even better products.					
(vii) We have a person in our organization who constantly monitors whether changes in the market have changed the value driver of our strategy.					

CHAPTER 9

Ideas for Green Growth Strategies

> When green is all there is to be,
> It could make you wonder why.
> But why consider, why wonder?
> I am green, and it'll do fine.
> And I think it's what I want to be.
> — Kermit in *It's Not Easy Being Green: And Other Things to Consider* by Jim Henson

Green growth strategies have to do with *innovation*. Not incremental improvements like in the Red quadrant; rather, it's the big jumps, the products and services that break away from the pack. It is about creativity, change, new perspectives, and "creative destruction." It's about breakthrough new ideas (see Figure 9.1).

The 2008 Beijing Olympics turned out to be a showcase for various innovations. From a 12-petal lotus-flower-shaped tennis center and bicycles with frames made from a single piece of carbon fiber to lighter volleyballs made of microfiber rather than leather, various companies displayed impressive innovations. These were the results of pushing their R&D teams to come up with cool new ideas to help Olympians break records. And, of course, help to draw consumers to their products.[1]

---

[1] See "The Olympics and Innovation" *Business Week*, August 18, 2008.

From *www.gizmodo.com*

From *www.bicycle.net*

See *www.andrewlacerenza.blogspot.com*

FIGURE 9.1
The Beijing 2008 Olympics showcased new ideas from four companies' R&D departments.

Courtesy of Cary Wolinsky.

FIGURE 9.2
The BIG SQUEEZE is on as the world's population mushrooms, incomes rise, and freshwater resources diminish.

Opportunities for innovation are everywhere. Take water, for example. Global freshwater resources are currently threatened by rising demands from many quarters (see Figure 9.2). Population growth is one. Each of us needs a minimum of 1000 cubic meters of water per year for drinking, hygiene, and growing food.[2] That is, 40% of the size

---

[2] See Peter Rogers, "Facing the Freshwater Crisis," *Scientific American*, August 2008, pp. 46–53.

of an Olympic swimming pool. Climate change is another factor that's threatening the water supply; there are more droughts.

The challenge is figuring out how to supply water without degrading the natural ecosystems that provide it. It is likely that governments will begin to invest in the infrastructure for water conservation and ways to boost water supply, such as desalination.

What kind of innovation opportunities is the looming global water-shortage crisis likely to create? Quite a few. One is more efficient (and possibly portable) desalination and/or water purification equipment. Perhaps even something small enough that an individual can carry to convert any kind of water anywhere into something potable.

Another is technologies to conserve irrigation flows to conserve significantly more fresh water. A third is raising crop yields, so more crops can be harvested with less water. Companies like Monsanto are already working on this.

A fourth idea is developing products and services that can channel water eventually intended for crop fields to underground storage in the non-growing season. An interesting reality is that rainfall, snow accumulation, and runoff to rivers reach their peaks during nongrowing seasons in most parts of the world. This creates a supply-demand imbalance. Supply is at its highest when demand is relatively low. Developing effective storage facilities underground can help attenuate this.

The list of possibilities goes on and on. Low-water sanitation, a very useful innovation, has enormous growth potential. For example, Stockholm is experimenting with a system that operates on waste matter like a garden composter. It first separates excrement from urine. One part is used as liquid farm fertilizer; the rest is recycled into fertilizer by microorganisms in a compost bin.

A lot of money is going to be spent on this problem in the future. A Booz Allen Hamilton estimate is that governments around the world will need to spend $1 trillion a year on applying existing technologies for conserving water, maintaining and replacing infrastructure, and constructing sanitation systems. Attractive prospects emerge from this for engineering consulting firms, such as CH2M Hill in Denver, or beer companies thinking of getting into branded bottled drinking water.

In the past decade, the perceived returns on innovation have gone up substantially. Why? Three reasons. First, the approach of improving value creation through greater cost productivity, efficiency, and quality that was so popular in the 1980s and 1990s has run its course as a *source of competitive advantage*.

Think about the Toyota example we discussed in previous chapters. Clearly, if your organization is not as good as the best in class as far as productivity, efficiency, and quality go, your chances of survival in a competitive industry are diminished. But we are at a stage where most companies in any given industry have harvested most of the gains available from (Red) efficiency initiatives like Six-Sigma and Lean-Sigma.

Second, most companies have discovered that growing through M&A is hardly a panacea. Acquisitions undertaken during the 1990s have fared no better than those undertaken earlier. Companies are beginning to realize that organic growth may be a better option than acquisitions in many instances.

Third, the capital market demands growth. If growth is not going to come from acquisitions, then it has to arise organically. And innovation can be the wellspring of organic growth.

GREEN'S BREAKTHROUGH IDEAS

What Is Innovation?

Innovation is a process that:

- Enhances something—think of Google, which enhanced how we search for information.

- Obsolesces something—think of the automobile (which made the buggy whip obsolete) or CDs, which made records obsolete.

- Surfaces latent needs—think of GPS in cars, which made drivers satisfy a latent need for directions.

- Creates a resource out of what was never a resource—think of silicon chips, which made sand a resource. Think of land—the Native Americans never viewed it as resource; it was the game they could hunt on the land that they viewed as a resource. Farming technology made land a resource.

Why Is Innovation So Difficult?

Typical attitudes act as an impediment. These are a few familiar ones:

- Innovation doesn't pay in my business.

- Innovation isn't my job . . . that's left up to those in the R&D department.

- My boss doesn't value innovation.

- My firm doesn't appreciate innovation.

- Who's got the time? I am up to my eyeballs in work already!

DOES INNOVATION HAVE ANY GENERALIZABLE PRINCIPLES?

> There are no rules; and those are the rules.
> – **Cantus Fraggle in *It's Not Easy Being Green* by Jim Henson**

Most people think of innovation the way Cantus Fraggle does in the Muppets. This, however, is not quite true. There are a number of principles (see Figure 9.3), as I discuss in the following subsections.

Principle 1: Combine and Hitchhike to Innovate

What do the innovative products in Figure 9.4 have in common? The Tweel airless tire is the first real innovation in tires since the Michelin brothers invented tires in the nineteenth century. Not only is the tire (virtually) airless, but it is also capable of individual optimization of vertical and lateral stiffness.

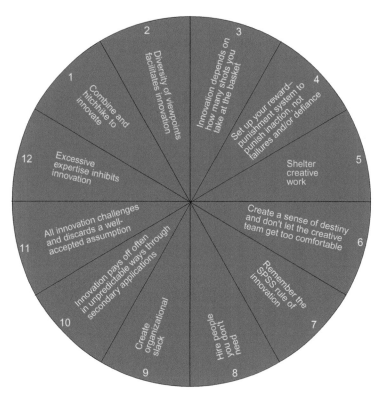

FIGURE 9.3
The CVF principles of innovation.

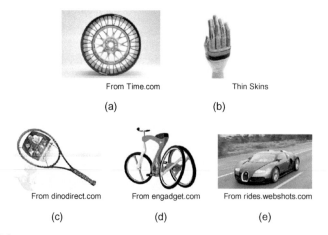

From Time.com   Thin Skins

(a)   (b)

From dinodirect.com   From engadget.com   From rides.webshots.com

(c)   (d)   (e)

FIGURE 9.4
Examples of innovative products: (a) the Tweel airless tire, (b) Thin Skins by the University of Tokyo, (c) the
Fischer magnetic speed tennis racket, (d) the Shift 164 tricycle, and (e) the 2007 Bugatti Veyron.

This contrasts with the joint optimization of these two forms of stiffness that must be done at present, which forces tradeoffs. These tradeoffs can be avoided in the Tweel. Currently used only for wheel chairs and ambulatory equipment in hospitals, the upside growth potential of this innovation is sky high.

Thin Skins is a glove made out of thin plastic film with embedded sensors. The sensors permit the glove to sense heat and pressure. Pretty much like human skin. Potential applications are almost endless— from giving robots a sense of touch and feel to equipping car seats, carpets, and upholstery with these sensors so as to trigger lighting, cooling, and so on, in response to a person entering the room. If you can imagine an application, it's possible.

The Fischer magnetic speed tennis racquet is equipped with equally polarized magnets at 3 o'clock and 6 o'clock. These allow the racquet surface to return to its original position almost instantaneously after contact with the ball, which generates tremendous power in ground strokes.

The Shift tricycle, an invention of two Purdue engineering professors, combines the best of a bicycle and a tricycle. At low speeds, it works like a tricycle, as the rear wheels spread out. This provides the needed balance at low speeds. As the rider speeds up, the rear wheels come together and it becomes a bicycle.

Finally, Veyron is Bugatti's new supercar. Produced by Volkswagen, it is the fastest production automobile in the world. Equipped with a 1001-horsepower, 16-cylinder, quad-turbocharged engine, the car has a top speed of 253 mph. And it goes from 0 to 60 in a blinding 2.5 seconds! All you need is the ability to afford a $1.6 million car.

At first blush, these inventions have little in common. But note that none of them is an entirely new invention, a complete break from the past. Each uses a *combination* of technologies that were already in place.

This is actually one of the most successful ways to innovate. Combining things that already exist often produces remarkable new products and services.

From visualphotos.com

Look around your organization, your industry, and other industries. What things that already exist in different organizations or industries can be combined to yield new products or new services?

Principle 2: Diversity of Viewpoints Facilitates Innovation

Innovation happens in different ways, just as people are creative in different ways (see Figure 9.5). Thus, there is no "formula" for innovation. Because innovation has such breathtaking diversity, having a workforce with a diversity of viewpoints spurs innovation. Diversity not only serves different types of situations, but also produces the creative tension necessary for innovation. Creative diversity is a key to gaining strategic advantage and substantial value creation.

Some of the most creative organizations around—Ideo, W. L. Gore, firms in Silicon Valley—employ eclectic groups of people with varied

FIGURE 9.5
The parent–child organization also has rules for strategies.
Courtesy of Jeffrey Koterba from *compsci.ca/blog; used with permission.*

backgrounds and from a multitude of disciplines. In fact, more than half the entrepreneurs funded by Silicon Valley in the past decade were born outside this country. Think, for example, of the founders of Google, Intel, and many others.

Principle 3: Innovation Depends on How Many Shots You Take at the Basket

Research has shown that the success of innovation depends on the *quantity* of ideas generated. Just like a basketball player who must take a lot of three-point shots to make a few, innovators need to try a lot of new ideas to find breakthrough innovations. The reason is that innovation is an inherently risky business. To come up with an innovative idea that works, you have to *generate a lot of ideas*, both good and bad.

This then generates a wide range of options that can be combined (see Principle 1) to create even more innovations. When one focuses on a single blockbuster innovation, the pursuit is that of perfection rather than experimentation. This is rarely successful. It is experimentation that often leads to successful innovation.

Principle 4: Set Up Your Reward–Punishment System to Punish Inaction, Not Failure and/or Defiance

If you want people to take more shots at the basket, then your evaluation system must reward that. How? Don't punish defiance—just inaction. In fact, creative people don't always conform. They don't always obey the rules.

People who do what they think is right—rather than what they are told or what they anticipate their superiors want—can drive their bosses crazy and get their companies in deep trouble. But it is precisely these kinds of people you need to innovate. This exposes a sharp contrast between the obey-the-rules types you need for Red initiatives and the types you need for Green.

In *The HP Way*, David Packard brags about an employee who defied a direct order from him. "Some years ago, at an HP lab in Colorado

Springs devoted to oscilloscope technology, one of our bright, energetic engineers, Chuck House, was advised to abandon a display monitor he was developing. Instead he embarked on a vacation to California—stopping along the way to show potential customers a prototype."

House persisted with the project, eventually persuading his R&D manager to rush the monitor into production. The product was a big success. Packard: "Some years later, at a gathering of HP engineers, I presented Chuck with a medal for extraordinary contempt and defiance beyond the normal call of engineering duty." To encourage this sort of behavior, there is a need to reward *both* success and failure.

Why? The reason is that it is impossible to generate a few good ideas without also generating a lot of bad ideas. So the organization should punish only inaction. Inaction is the kiss of death for an organization that wants creativity.

Picasso, Da Vinci, Richard Feynman (astrophysicist and Nobel Prize winner), and Einstein did not always succeed at a higher rate than their peers. They produced more. That means they had more successes and failures than their colleagues. The bottom line is this: Creativity is often a function of the quantity of work produced (more shots at the basket mean more creativity).

Those engaged in creative enterprises recognize this. Consider Jim Henson, creator of the Muppets:

> Creatively, I find I work best if I can work with someone—talking things over as ideas come up. I do this best with people I'm very comfortable with—there has to be an absolutely pressure-free situation for this to work well. Jerry Juhl and I have always been able to work this way. It's important to be able to say virtually anything—which may be totally silly or stupid or obscene—in a no-risk situation.
> **– Jim Henson in *It's Not Easy Being Green***

Principle 5: Shelter Creative Work

Innovation is fragile—it can be lost even with the best of intentions. Particularly if it is closely monitored the way one should monitor Red initiatives. William Coyne, former VP of R&D at 3M said it best: "After you plant a seed in the ground, you don't dig it up every week to see how it is doing." To develop new products and services, keep your creative people away from your biggest customers—or from critics or anyone whose primary concern is money.

As W. Edwards Deming said, "The last thing you should do is to ask your customers what new products they want, or to ask your students what you should teach them." The point is: Exposing creative work to premature criticism can kill it. A major problem is that "proving" that an innovation will work is often very hard. The usual approach of collecting more data to improve decision-making doesn't work. In fact, asking for more data to move forward in innovation is often an act of resistance to action.

Often, the only solution is to commit wholeheartedly to the project despite slim odds of success. As sociologist Robert Merton said:

> The self-fulfilling prophecy is, in the beginning, a false definition of the situation evoking a new behavior which makes the originally false conception come true. A specious validity of the self-fulfilling prophecy perpetuates a reign of error. For the prophet will cite the actual course of events as proof that he was right from the very beginning. Such are the perversities of social logic.

Principle 6: Create a Sense of Destiny and Don't Let the Creative Team Get Too Comfortable

Just because innovation has to be sheltered does not mean the creative team should be allowed to feel too comfortable. You have to create a sense of destiny, but then you get people to fight with each other about ideas, not personalities. Every idea should be challengeable, not people.

A good example of this is provided by Bob Taylor, psychologist and administrator at the U.S. Department of Defense's Advanced Research Projects Agency (ARPA) in the 1960s and later at Xerox in the 1970s. Computer scientists Taylor funded through ARPA meet at an annual series of research conferences.

Michael Hilzik describes the interactions as follows:

> The daily discussions unfolded in a pattern that remained peculiar to Taylor's management style throughout his career. Each participant got an hour or so to describe his work. Then he would be thrown to the mercy of the assembled court like a flank steak to a pack of ravenous wolves.

Taylor himself stated:

> I got them to argue with each other. These were people who cared about their work... if there were technical weak spots, they would almost always surface under these conditions. It was very, very healthy.

Remember: Creativity loves restraint. Give people a vision, rules about how to get there, and deadlines. If you don't set boundaries and deadlines, innovation can go on forever. It's a messy process!

Principle 7: Remember the SPSS Rule of Innovation

The idea is that innovation in an organization must have a strategy that is supported by organizational resources—obviously. Surprisingly, you also need an innovation process. (See Figure 9.6.)

The SPSS of Innovation	
Strategy	• Not every innovative idea has to be a blockbuster. Great innovations come about from combinations of known things. • Innovation is not just about products.
Process	• Tight controls strangle innovation because one size does not fit all. • Expect deviations from the plan and shelter creative ideas early.
Structure	• Loosen controls but tighten interpersonal connections between innovation efforts and the rest of the business (e.g., Wabash National and Reuters).
Skills	• Innovations need strong leaders with good communication skills who tolerate defiance and reward both successes and failures. • Innovations need connectors—people who know how to find partners in the mainstream business.

FIGURE 9.6

Innovation involves strategy, process, structure, and skills—the SPSS rule.

Even though process is a Red practice, without an innovation process, the organization will be too dependent on the creativity of specific individuals. It will not be able to sustain innovation. But an innovation process is very different from an auditing or a manufacturing process. It has a structure, but permits a lot of freelancing within the process. There is considerable autonomy and an absence of tight controls.

Innovation also needs the right organizational structure that connects innovators to the mainstream business. Innovative companies know this all too well. Consider the following statement by CTO Sophie Vandebroek, Xerox's "inventor-in-chief":

> Within research you play three roles. There's an explorer role, where we push the limits of the technology and constantly look at how we can come up with these bright new ideas, either within the company or working with partners. Then we have the partnership role. You work with the business-group engineers to make sure these cool technologies actually end up in a product or a service. The third role, in the middle, is the incubator. Some of these novel technologies might work in the labs, but before the business groups will take them on you need to make sure no more invention is required. In this phase we try to understand fully the business value of these ideas and incubate them to a level where the business group says, "Yes, I want to invest in that."

Principle 8: Hire People You Don't Need

Innovation needs diverse viewpoints. Why? Because *what* we see in any given situation depends on our *beliefs* prior to the observation. A diversity of beliefs allows us to see more possibilities. The more diverse the workforce, the more diverse the beliefs.

Diversity is important because it is not easy to predict what viewpoints we will need for future innovation. That is, since innovation means we are creating things we cannot predict before the fact, we also cannot predict precisely the set of skills and viewpoints we will need for the (future) innovation.

This, in turn, implies that we may have to hire people we *don't* really have a need for at present. People like anthropologists, ethnographers, sociologists, and psychologists. That's exactly the kind of people Xerox Research Centers hire. So do other innovative firms like Ideo.

Recognize again the tension between this practice and the efficiency demanded by Red. Hiring people you "don't need" doesn't help cost productivity!

Principle 9: Create Organizational Slack

One real-world impediment to innovation in organizations is the lack of organizational *slack*. Resources are so efficiently deployed that no one can spare the time for anything but their designated job. In such organizations, innovation is very difficult. There is often frustration because nothing of substance really happens.

To get around this, the organization has to explicitly and deliberately create slack. Expect employees to spend a certain percentage of their time (say 20%) on generating new ideas (see Figure 9.7). Reward those who generate new ideas. W. L. Gore does this. The company expects its employees to spend some of their time on thinking of new product ideas that are applications of the company's existing portfolio of core technologies.

Recognize that slack is the enemy of efficiency. Thus, an organization dedicated to being an excellent Red will find it particularly challenging to endorse and adopt this principle. This is another illustration of the tension between initiatives in opposite quadrants.

From eschoolnews.com

FIGURE 9.7

This group of students may look like they are not studying, but actually they are cooperating to create a new idea.

Principle 10: Innovation Pays Off, Often in Unpredictable Ways through Secondary Applications

Adopters of innovation are also diverse and unpredictable, so it is difficult to predict how an innovation will take off. Often the "standard" rules of capital budgeting and resource allocation produce exactly the wrong prescription. They generate negative Net Present Values (NPV) when they are applied to innovative projects. And consequently, these projects often do not survive the usual capital budgeting screens.

The mistake in applying the NPV rule to Green projects is the assumption that if the organization did not undertake the Green project, the status quo of zero NPV would prevail. But if you don't take the project and your competitor does, how good is your status quo assumption? (See Figure 9.8.)

Normal capital budgeting (Red and Blue projects) involves the usual diminishing marginal returns to scale. Capital is rationed, and projects with negative returns (or negative NPVs) are denied capital.

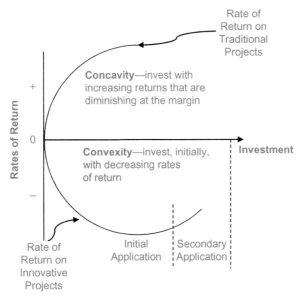

FIGURE 9.8
Rates of return on innovation.

But Green projects are different. Many of them are characterized by negative initial returns that get worse. In fact, if one only focuses on the initial application of the innovation, then the project may be difficult to justify. Quite often, what makes the project really attractive is the *secondary* application, and it is that which makes the returns start moving up sharply. 3M's Post-it notes and Pfizer's Viagra are both examples of products that found their greatest revenue potential in applications for which they were *not* initially designed.

Think of flat-screen monitors. The technology was first invented by Westinghouse Electric Corporation in Pennsylvania. But Westinghouse did not view it as attractive enough to justify investing in developing it. Why? There was no way to reliably predict all of its future uses and hence profitability. The early patents were bought by the Japanese, who exhibited the patience to wait for secondary and tertiary applications. The first profitable application was to personal computers. But the real bonanza was to come later, when the technology was used for television!

Another example is the Global Positioning Satellite (GPS) technology (see Figure 9.9). Developed initially for military applications, the really high returns on investing in this technology did not come until OnStar used it for automobiles.

These are examples of innovations that eventually paid off. But before the secondary and tertiary applications were evident, it was difficult to predict that these would arrive. For every innovation that is associated

From USAF Research Laboratory

FIGURE 9.9
Defense satellite communications systems.

with profitable secondary and tertiary applications, there are dozens that are busts. The risks are high.

However, risk taking is the essence of Green growth strategies. It's also what distinguishes these strategies from Red strategies in the diagonally opposite quadrant. Red seeks stability. Red seeks risk minimization. Green seeks "organized chaos." Green seeks experimentation. And experiments are often risky.

To quote Kirk to the crew in *Star Trek*, "Return to Tomorrow":

> Risk is our business. That's what this starship is all about. That's why we are aboard her.
> **– From *The Quotable Star Trek* by Jill Sherwin**

The mind set you have to develop to launch Green growth strategies is to generate a large *portfolio* of ideas, expecting that the majority of them will fail. But what you are banking on is that a couple will turn out to be spectacular hits! That is the mindset of a venture capitalist.

Principle 11: All Innovation Challenges and Discards a Well-Accepted Assumption—Rule? Truth?

One of the reasons why innovation is difficult is that we make similar assumptions, or obey similar "rules." The result is that we think alike. These common assumptions and rules define the "business paradigm" everybody follows. Break one of these assumptions and you create a new paradigm. Just the way Starbucks did with coffee; the way Toyota did with automobiles; the way eBay did with online auctions.

This view is exemplified by Bonnie Bassler, McArthur Young Genius Award-winning microbiologist at Princeton: "I always start with the premise that everything we know is wrong. And my greatest gift to my students is that by the time I am done with them, they believe it too." What assumptions do you accept as "truths" in your business? Which can you drop to create a new business paradigm?

Every day, creative people are dropping well-accepted assumptions to innovate. For example, for a long time, people assumed that you could

Photo by Gregg Segal

FIGURE 9.10
Martin Eberhard, pictured with the Tesla in 2007.

not have an all-electric car that used *no* gas, drove fast, and was fun to drive. Yet a man named Martin Eberhard has developed precisely such a car (see Figure 9.10). It is called Tesla. It is a 2650-pound vehicle with a carbon-fiber body and a lithium ion battery back.[3] It is a rear-wheel-drive roadster that can go 220 miles on a single charge. It has a top speed of 125 mph. And it goes from 0 to 60 in an eye-popping 3.9 seconds!

It is far too early to tell whether Tesla will establish itself as a commercially successful product. It has financial backing as well as a waiting list of celebrity buyers. But its commercial launch has been delayed a few times. The reasons are classic in the context of the CVF. The product was developed by a Green visionary—Eberhard. It was backed by a financier named Elon Musk. Given that the product is on hand, what is needed now for commercial launch is the expertise of a good Red.

Perhaps for this reason, Musk replaced Eberhard as CEO with Michael Marks, former CEO of Flextronics and a minority investor in Tesla. Marks was supposedly a manufacturing whiz who insists on cost efficiency and sticking to schedules. Marks was later replaced by Ze'ev Drori, an operations-focused veteran. Eberhard was ousted from the Board in 2007 and 10% of the workforce was laid off.

---

[3] See Michael V. Copeland, "Tesla's Wild Ride," *Fortune*, July 21, 2008.

Nonetheless, the first batch of Teslas have rolled off the line. But the volume of production at present is minuscule compared to what the company will need to be a real car company. Numerous uncertainties—mostly having to do with the reliability of the battery technology—remain. Like all innovations, it's risky. But someday we may look back and say it was the start of a revolution in the automobile industry.

Tesla is an example of a product innovation. There is also a lot of value-creation potential in *paradigm innovation*. A paradigm is simply a set of assumptions about how the company interacts with various stakeholders—customers, suppliers, employees, and investors—and how it delivers its products and services.

The power of new paradigm—and the process by which these are created—is underappreciated. Organizations tend to focus far more on inventing new products and services. Yet the profits to be harvested from new paradigms—new ways of doing business even with the *same* products and services—often far exceed those from new products and services.

Think about it. Starbucks created a new paradigm, not a new product. Dell, with its direct-sale business model, created a new paradigm. It did not create a new product. Barnes & Noble, too, created a new paradigm.

Principle 12: Excessive Expertise Inhibits Innovation

Another impediment to innovation is expertise: That a mob is better than a lone genius all too often is not true. When we know "too much" about a product, a service, or a market, it actually becomes more difficult to innovate. The relationship between creativity and knowledge looks something like that shown in Figure 9.11.

Why does creativity first increase and then decline with knowledge beyond a certain point? The reason is simple. You need a certain amount of knowledge first before you can innovate. Martin Eberhard could not have invented the Tesla without knowing quite a bit about cars and electricity. But as you accumulate more and more knowledge, your mind becomes "socialized" in the assumptions of the existing paradigm.

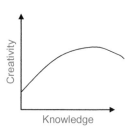

FIGURE 9.11
Creativity versus knowledge.

The distinction between assumptions and facts becomes blurred. You take the existing assumptions as inviolable rules. You think like everybody else. To innovate, you have to assume that the status quo is *wrong*. This is the mindset one needs to innovate. In fact, this may well be the reason why some of the most innovative ideas may be brought to you by people outside your organization.

THE PROCESS OF INNOVATION

Although innovation is Green, the *process* of innovation involves all four quadrants. This is shown in Figure 9.12. Every great innovative organization has an innovation process. And while the details may vary, the essential elements of the innovation process will include what is described in the figure.

It all starts with putting the right team together. The team leader at this stage, a stage called *Incubate Cooperating*, should be a good Yellow. Cooperation, establishing a culture of process for learning, and putting in place the necessary team dynamics all occur in this stage.

Then comes the *Imagine Inventing* phase, which is Green. There has to be a process for gathering data and brainstorming ideas for new products, services, and markets.

The third phase, which is Blue, is called *Invest in Competing*. This is when you commit resources. You create the initiatives, ventures, and partnerships to make the product commercially viable.

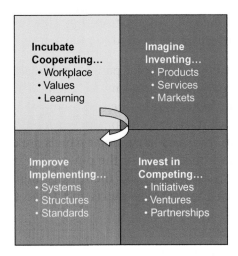

FIGURE 9.12
CVF and the innovation process.

Finally, *Improve Implementing* is the Red phase. This is the stage in which you reexamine your systems, structures, and processes to improve them. You develop and refine standards. You document what you learned, both from your failures and from your successes. You put in place the mechanisms to make the innovation process *replicable*. The innovation process at Ideo, perhaps the leading product design firm in the world, has these elements.

SOME THOUGHTS ON INNOVATION OPPORTUNITIES FOR THE FUTURE

In its December 2009 issue, *Scientific American* discussed 20 "world-changing ideas." I discuss a few of them in the subsections that follow to illustrate the enormous future potential of innovation. I invite you to add your own ideas to the list.

Solar Panels

If large enough solar panels are installed on a rooftop, enough energy can be produced to power the entire house. An important impediment is that solar panels are expensive and typically unaffordable for many.

However, a recent *financing* innovation may solve this problem. With this innovation, investors are invited to put their money into a pool.

This pool is used to purchase solar panels for households. Households that install these panels pay nothing for them. The households purchase the electricity generated by the solar panels in their own homes, but pay less than what they would pay for electricity from the grid. So consumers benefit. Investors in the solar panels are compensated from the payments from households for the power they consume. This provides them the necessary return on their investment. Can this financing approach be used for other products and services?

Gasoline Garden

In July 2009, Exxon Mobil announced plans to spend more than $600 million in research on genetically engineered algae that produce hydrocarbons as a by-product of their normal metabolism. If successful, this will produce common gasoline using nothing but sunlight and CO_2. How will this change the world? What opportunities will this open up for your organization?

Wind Power from the Stratosphere

A study by Stanford University released in July 2009 indicated that the high-altitude winds that blow tens of thousands of feet above our planet hold *enough energy to support all of human civilization 100 times over*! A company from California, Sky Windpower, has proposed a way to harvest this energy: fleets of giant, airborne, ground-tethered windmills. What will this do to the prices of different types of fuels? What kinds of new industries will this spawn if successful?

Ubiquitous Sensors

During 2009, Hewlett-Packard announced the launch of its Central Nervous System for the Earth (CeNSE) project. This is a 10-year effort to embed up to a trillion pushpin-size sensors across the planet. These versatile sensors, or "motes," will transmit information about the Earth that will enhance our understanding of nature. But it promises much more.

We could have buildings that manage their own energy use, bridges that tell engineers when they are in need of repair, and cars that detect traffic patterns and potholes! Besides Hewlett-Packard, Intel and numerous university labs are developing new sensor packages. What growth opportunities will this create for your organization?

Bacterial Toothpaste

A company in Florida, Oragenics, has genetically engineered a new strain of bacteria that converts sugars in a person's mouth into alcohol. The bacteria permanently displace natural *Streptococcus mutans*, the bacteria in the mouth that causes tooth decay. When developed, this innovation will result in a one-time prescription that will protect teeth for life.

The preceding are just a few of the many innovations that are being developed. They have transformational potential. They will create new threats for some and a continent of opportunities for others.

LESSONS

The lessons you take away from this chapter truly depend on your perspective. But here are some that stand out in my mind:

- Innovation can often be the wellspring of explosive organic growth. But innovation is hard because of everyday attitudes and lack of organizational "slack" to devote to innovation.

- There are numerous principles of innovation. The key one to remember is that it takes a vast amount of experimentation to generate a few good ideas, so your organizational culture and metrics have to be geared to encouraging people to work on generating a lot of ideas—both good and bad. Failure should not be punished. It should be viewed as a source of *learning* and rewarded. Only inaction should be discouraged.

- Innovation often pays in the future through secondary and tertiary applications. Financial returns on initial applications are often disappointing. This frequently results in promising ideas being abandoned.

- All innovation discards an assumption that all players in the industry take as a given.

- All innovative organizations have a process for innovation that includes all four quadrants of the CVF.

- There are some incredible innovations in the works that will change our society in profound ways. Even if your organization is not directly involved in these innovations, it may be able to benefit from the numerous growth opportunities that will arise due to the changes brought about by these innovations.

Reflection Exercise

As a leader in your organization, please choose a number from 1 to 5 to assign to each statement in Exercise 9.1.

Exercise 9.1
1 = Strongly disagree; 2 = Disagree; 3 = Neither agree nor disagree; 4 = Agree; 5 = Strongly agree

	1	2	3	4	5
(i) We have an innovative organization.					
(ii) Our business paradigm relies on discarding a key assumption (which is: _____) that everybody else in our industry uses.					
(iii) Our organization celebrates both the successes and failures in our innovation efforts.					
(iv) We have the appropriate organizational "slack" for innovation.					
(v) We often hire people with eclectic backgrounds with skills that we currently don't need.					
(vi) We focus our innovation efforts primarily on coming up with new products and services.					
(vii) We have someone who thinks about how our existing business model could be made obsolete and the new paradigm that could replace it.					

- As in previous chapters, have various groups in your organization go through this exercise as well.

- Does this exercise suggest any action steps for your organization?

CHAPTER 10

Wrapping Up

> There was neither nonexistence nor existence then;
> there was neither the realm of space nor the sky which
> is beyond. What stirred? Where? In whose protection?
> Was there water, bottomlessly deep?
> — Nāsadīya in *The Rig Veda*, as translated
> by Wendy Doniger O'Flaherty

In this book we have examined the four growth strategies that organizations can employ to grow the top line. We color-coded these strategies: Yellow, Red, Blue, and Green (see Figure 10.1). Each of the four quadrants has its virtues. And its negative zone too, if you take it too far and drift to the extremes.

If an organization does not have enough Yellow in its culture, it will die a slow death. But if it has too much, it will go to the negative zone and be like a country club: a lot of fun but not much getting done.

If an organization does not have enough Green, it will stagnate. But if it has too much, it will be like a chaotic research lab. Lots of activity and ideas, but no closure and no commercially viable products or services.

If an organization does not have enough Blue, it becomes uncompetitive, irrelevant, and doomed to extinction. But if it has too much Blue, it becomes a sweatshop.

141

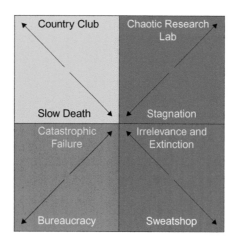

FIGURE 10.1
Too much or too little of any color hurts.

If an organization has insufficient Red, it can experience catastrophic failure. But too much Red can make it a stifling bureaucracy.

INTERPENETRATION OF OPPOSITES: EMBRACING THE PARADOX

Although at the first level, the Competing Values Framework (CVF) points to the tensions that exist between diagonally opposite quadrants, an elemental truth is that the best-in-class are able to embrace the paradox. Achieve an interpenetration of opposites. That means developing a strong growth strategy in one quadrant but using the tools of the diagonally opposite quadrant to enhance it.

The first insight of the CVF is that this is difficult to do because the diagonally opposite quadrants are competing forms of value creation (see Figure 10.2). This is why it endows the organization with a core competence and a competitive advantage when it can be done. It is a core competence in part because it is difficult to imitate.

Take Ideo, for example. Located in Palo Alto, California, it is the most influential product design firm in the world. It designs over 100 new

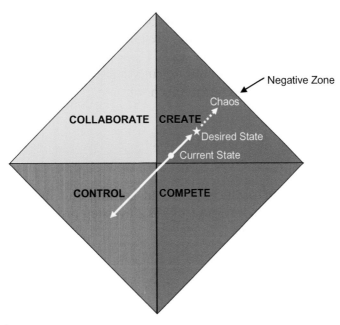

FIGURE 10.2
Interpenetration of opposites: a tool to prevent drifting to the negative zone.

products a year, for customers as diverse as Nike, Apple, and the film industry. Ideo is a quintessential Green. However, it has a sophisticated process of innovation that everybody in the organization embraces.

In fact, Ideo is proud of saying that it doesn't care what product design it is innovating. What matters is that it is able to apply its *process* to the innovation. So here's a company whose business and growth strategy are Green, and yet it defines its core competence in terms of a process, something we associate with Red.

General Dynamics, which we discussed in Chapter 8, is another example. When faced with declining industry prospects in 1991, the company downsized dramatically, shrinking in sales from $9.5 billion to $3.2 billion—a classic Blue initiative. But in the midst of dealing with a Blue crisis with a Blue initiative, General Dynamics paid striking attention to Yellow. Its CEO, Bill Anders, asked his COO, James Mellon, to spend most of his time for a period of six months simply teaching the General Dynamics' managers what it really meant to manage for cash.

How do you run the business differently if managing cash flow is a key goal? Knowledge and teaching are part of Yellow. He significantly reshuffled his top management team. He reengineered the compensation structure. He sent his senior executives for an executive education program for week at a top business school.

DESIGNING AND IMPLEMENTING A GROWTH STRATEGY

How does your organization go about crafting and implementing a growth strategy? Given in Figure 10.3 is a five-step process that is based on our earlier discussions.

FIGURE 10.3
A Growth Strategy formulation.

We have discussed ① and ② shown in the figure extensively. As for ③, the white spaces are untapped opportunities that exist in the gaps between your existing products and services. So it is not about what you are doing today. It's more about what you *could* do. It is Coca-Cola getting into bottled water.

As for ④, it is important to conduct a careful diagnosis of whether your corporate culture is aligned with your growth strategy. Are the metrics, processes, and behaviors aligned with achieving the Blue, Red, or Yellow growth that your strategy is designed to achieve? The CVF cultural diagnostic tools can help here.

Finally, ⑤ addresses the Green component of your Growth Strategy. Green is all about trying a lot of experiments—a large diversity of experiments to generate a few good ideas.

- What kind of organizational slack have you created for innovation?
- How do you assess the success of innovation?
- How do you reward and/or incentivize innovation?

CONCLUDING MESSAGE

> No wants. No needs. We weren't meant for that. None of us. Man stagnates if he has no ambition, no desire to be more than he is.
>
> **– Kirk to Spock in "This Side of Paradise"**
> **in *The Quotable Star Trek* by Jill Sherwin**

So my concluding message is simply this. Growth is essential for any organization. The alternative to growth is stagnation.

Make a choice and formulate a specific growth strategy. The choice means deciding which quadrant of the CVF will dominate your growth strategy. This color-codes your growth strategy.

Then express it in simple terms (two bullet points). Recognize the CVF tensions in your growth strategy. Conduct a systematic diagnosis of your current and your preferred culture to execute the growth strategy.

Then proceed to realign the organization to the preferred culture by adapting your metrics and processes. Identify the behaviors that need to be reinforced, and those that need to be eliminated and/or changed.

As you do all this, make sure to communicate the strategy and the behaviors you wish to discourage and encourage. Communicate, communicate, communicate!

Remember you can create value with any of these growth strategies. As a leader in your organization, the CVF can serve as a compass to support your company's good growth.

Reflection Exercise

As your organization's leader, please choose a number from 1 to 5 to assign to each statement in Exercise 10.1.

Exercise 10.1
1 = Strongly disagree; 2 = Disagree; 3 = Neither agree nor disagree; 4 = Agree; 5 = Strongly agree

	1	2	3	4	5
(i) We have a well-articulated growth strategy.					
(ii) We know the color of our growth strategy.					
(iii) We reinforce our growth strategy by communicating it to the organization at least once a week.					
(iv) We understand how our corporate culture needs to evolve to support our growth strategy.					
(v) We are actively working on adapting our culture to our growth strategy.					
(vi) We often hire people with eclectic backgrounds with skills that we currently don't need.					
(vii) We focus our innovation efforts primarily on coming up with new products and services.					
(viii) We have someone who thinks about how our existing business model could be made obsolete and the new paradigm that could replace it.					

Step 1: Have a group of your senior executives in the organization go through all the assessments in the previous chapters, and the Exercise 10.1 assessment, and individually write down the key observations that emerge from this exercise.

Step 2: Break up the group into 3 to 5 teams to discuss their observations.

Step 3: Convene all the groups to present their findings and to share their observations.

Step 4: Break up into 3 to 5 teams again to discuss specific organizational change action steps stemming from the observations of all groups.

Step 5: Convene all the groups to present their findings and to select 3 to 5 key action steps for the organization. Make sure that there is at least one short-term, one medium-term, and one long-term change in the action steps.

The Competing Values Framework for Growth Strategy

This appendix provides a summary of the CVF for growth strategy. It examines how the various metrics for measuring value creation in each quadrant (Community and Knowledge in Yellow; Innovation and Growth in Green; Speed and Profits in Blue; and Efficiency and Quality in Red) relate to various aspects of value creation:

- Financial outcomes

- Organizational characteristics

- Organizational tendencies

- Organizational strengths

- Aspects of organizational culture

- Organizational leadership characteristics

- Culture blind spots for the organization

- Individual blind spots

Examining these aspects should help you to deepen your understanding of the CVF and the pros and cons of any specific growth strategy.

Performance metrics	Collaborate		Create	
	Community	Knowledge	Innovation	Growth
Operationalization of metrics—financial outcomes	Sales divided by the number of employees	Future growth values—the difference between the firm's current market value and its value if its profits do not grow	The standard deviation of the alpha in the firm's stock return—the difference between a company's actual returns and the portion of the returns that can be explained by co-movement with overall market return	Sales growth
Characteristics it sought	▪ Workforce commitment ▪ Shared values ▪ Inclusion ▪ Teamwork ▪ High-performing culture	▪ Workforce competence ▪ Continuous learning ▪ Employee retention ▪ Employee support ▪ Advancements in knowledge	▪ Product innovation ▪ Risk ▪ Exceptions ▪ Experimenting ▪ Change	▪ Capacity to change ▪ Risk ▪ Vision of possibility ▪ Exploration ▪ Transforming emerging trends
Tendencies	Internal capability and long-term development of culture	Adaptability and long-term development of culture	Adaptability and breakthrough transformation	Breakthrough transformation and external opportunities
Strengths through what is demanded	▪ Focus on internal maintenance ▪ People oriented ▪ Performance through shared values and inclusion ▪ Teamwork and consensus ▪ Developing culture over time	▪ Focus on internal maintenance ▪ People/process oriented ▪ Performance through new competencies ▪ Employee satisfaction ▪ Organizational development strategies	▪ Creative crisis to overturn the status quo ▪ Risk-seeking ▪ Demands flexibility and uniqueness ▪ Attracts entrepreneurship ▪ Seeks continual breakthroughs	▪ Demands future vision ▪ Focuses on new frontiers ▪ Creates ambiguity ▪ Succeeds through developing and testing scenarios ▪ Transforms opportunities

Compete		Control	
Speed	**Profits**	**Efficiency**	**Quality**
Change in firm's EVA growth rate from one year to next, over five-year period	Economic value added (EVA)—net operating profits after tax, minus capital charge, where capital charge equals firm's weighted-average cost of capital, times net assets deployed	Asset turnover—sales divided by assets in given year	Gross margin—price premium of higher quality products and services drives gross margin, as measured by sum of sales return, less cost of goods sold, divided by sales revenue
• Market share opportunities • Quick response • Domination • Aggressiveness	• Shareholder value • Predictable opportunities • Focus on competing • Short-term results • Managed resources	• Cost control • Regulation • Monitoring • Improvement • Stability	• Reliability • On-time delivery • Process improvement • Technical capability • Systems and technology
External opportunities and short-term performance	Short-term performance and stability	Stability and incremental improvement	Incremental improvement and internal capability
• Requires market analysis • Domination through acquisitions and alliances • Seeks skills to win • Compete-for-results culture	• Seeks stability through discipline • Focused goals lead to short-term results • Managed assets lead to shareholder value • Maximize bottom line • Attracts logic and predictability	• Policies and regulation drive improvements • Seeks better, faster, and cheaper • Data-driven standards • Monitor controls • Eliminate error and variation	• Systems and technology ensure quality • Superior capability through incremental improvement • Regular process review • Seeks stability • Smooth operations

(Continued)

Performance metrics	Collaborate		Create	
	Community	Knowledge	Innovation	Growth
Aspects of organizational culture	▪ Friendly atmosphere ▪ Participation ▪ Team goals ▪ Mentorship ▪ Shared values	▪ Information sharing ▪ Collaborative learning ▪ Dedicated masters-as-teachers ▪ Personal growth ▪ Long-term solution building ▪ Diversity ▪ Organizational development practices ▪ Employee retention	▪ Entrepreneurial ▪ Creative workplace ▪ Ongoing acquisition of new resources ▪ Individual freedoms ▪ Experimentation ▪ Ambiguity ▪ Risk	▪ Adventure ▪ Curiosity ▪ Emergent opportunities ▪ Clear vision ▪ Trend following ▪ Manage unknown
Organizational leadership characteristic	▪ Facilitator ▪ People oriented ▪ Consensus builder ▪ Tolerance for diversity ▪ Effective communicator	▪ Mentor ▪ Effective teacher ▪ Solution builder ▪ Tolerance for ideas ▪ Supportive	▪ Innovator ▪ Clever and creative ▪ Risk taker ▪ Learns from failure ▪ Experimenter ▪ Tolerance for ambiguity ▪ Abstract thinker	▪ Visionary ▪ Future oriented ▪ Visualizes new outcomes ▪ Opportunistic ▪ Intuitive ▪ Risk taker
Performance blind spots	Reluctant to assume that not all viewpoints are relevant or important	Reluctant to assume that correct people, values, and skills may already be in place	Reluctant to assume that continued success is possible by extending existing practices	Reluctant to assume that future is an extension of present

Compete		Control	
Speed	**Profits**	**Efficiency**	**Quality**
▪ Market domination ▪ Fast decision making ▪ Hard-driving ▪ Expansion of leadership power ▪ Leveraging of assets ▪ Mergers and acquisitions to speed up innovation ▪ Analytical	▪ Results-oriented ▪ Target-focused ▪ Demanding leadership ▪ Alignment of resources for specific purposes ▪ Managerial discipline ▪ Maximization of value ▪ Analytical ▪ Cost-competitive	▪ Structure ▪ Rules and policies ▪ Risk aversion ▪ Cost control ▪ Specialization of functions ▪ Task focus ▪ Preservation of order	▪ Improvement-focused ▪ Technology emphasis ▪ Best practices ▪ Workflow management ▪ Emphasis on troubleshooting ▪ Data focus ▪ Smooth operation ▪ Best-in-class focus
▪ Producer ▪ Task-focused ▪ Stealthy ▪ Aggressive and decisive ▪ Resourceful	▪ Competitor ▪ Aggressive and decisive ▪ Demanding ▪ Energizes employees ▪ Strategic ▪ Resourceful	▪ Administrator ▪ Technologically adept ▪ Conserves resources ▪ Standardizing ▪ Diligent	▪ Engineer ▪ Technologically adept ▪ Dependable and reliable ▪ Systems thinker ▪ Diligent ▪ Technical expert
Reluctance to assume that organization has capabilities necessary to enter new markets or to launch new products	Reluctance to assume that pursuit of immediate profits may jeopardize long-term sustainability	Reluctance to assume that laws, policies, and procedures can be circumnavigated	Reluctance to assume that operationalizing an idea at scale to achieve quality can be done without excessively detailed planning

(Continued)

Performance metrics	Collaborate		Create	
	Community	**Knowledge**	**Innovation**	**Growth**
Culture blind spots	▪ Issue avoidance ▪ Too participative ▪ Group think ▪ Too slow ▪ Too internal	▪ Forsake short term ▪ Inability to quickly respond ▪ Lack of critical feedback ▪ Too slow ▪ Too internal	▪ Too individualistic ▪ Lack of teamwork ▪ Superficiality over complexity	▪ Mismatched incentives ▪ Lack of loyalty
Individual blind spots	▪ Overemphasis on people and less task emphasis ▪ Cliquish ▪ Lack of metrics	▪ Knowledge doesn't always translate into practice ▪ Lack of focus ▪ Difficulty being direct	▪ Exhibits risky behavior ▪ Falls in love with ideas ▪ Micro-managing ▪ Inability to rally support	▪ Inability to produce viable ideas ▪ Disloyal to organization ▪ Micro-managing ▪ Fails to adjust personal ideas and won't satisfy other objectives
Examples—firm types	▪ Mission and/or advocacy-based organizations ▪ Associations ▪ Family businesses ▪ Lifestyle organizations ▪ Partnerships		▪ Mature firms in death cycle that need innovation to resurrect themselves ▪ Start-up firms ▪ Design and/or creative businesses	
Examples—specific firms	McKinsey	Ericsson	Google	Apple

Compete		Control	
Speed	**Profits**	**Efficiency**	**Quality**
▪ Pace is too fast ▪ Unnecessary competition ▪ Burnout	▪ Insufficient resources ▪ Unrealistic target setting ▪ Wasting of assets	▪ Too controlling ▪ Ideas don't develop ▪ Turf protection ▪ People ignored	▪ Too predictable ▪ Micro-management ▪ Distrust ▪ People ignored
▪ Takes easy route to quick fix ▪ Overly aggressive ▪ Too fast ▪ Bad with people	▪ Takes easy route to quick fix ▪ Myopic ▪ Unrealistic in demands ▪ Bad with people	▪ Overly analytical ▪ Lean and mean ▪ Blind to new ideas ▪ Lacks social skills	▪ Uses best practices as crutch ▪ Informs but won't teach ▪ Lacks social skills
▪ Large, diversified, public companies ▪ Financial institutions ▪ Leaders in large industries		▪ Operationally complex businesses ▪ Manufacturing firms ▪ Discount retailers ▪ Governments	
Microsoft	General Electric	Wal-Mart	Toyota

If you liked what you have read and want to learn more about how to use the Competing Values Framework for designing and implementing your growth strategy, please contact:

Dr. Anjan Thakor
Competing Values
734-604-1012
info@competingvalues.com

Resources and Additional Readings

Abel, Andrew B., "Optimal investment under uncertainty," *American Economic Review* 73(1), 228–233, 1983.

Aguerrevere, Felipe, "Equilibrium investment strategies and output price behavior: A real-options approach," *Review of Financial Studies* 16(4), 1239–1272, 2003.

Allen, Franklin, and Douglas Gale, *Financial Innovation and Risk Sharing.* Cambridge, MA: MIT Press, 1994.

Arrow, Kenneth, "Economic welfare and the allocation of resources for invention," in *The Rate and Direction of Inventive Activity* (ed., R.R. Nelson), pp. 609–625. Princeton, NJ: Princeton University Press, 1962.

Benjamin, John D., and C.F. Sirmans, "Pricing fixed rate mortgages: some empirical evidence," *Journal of Financial Services Research*, 4(3), 191–202, 1990.

Bitler, Marianne P., Tobias J. Moskowitz, and Annette Vissing-Jørgensen, "Testing agency theory with entrepreneur effort and wealth," *Journal of Finance* 60(2), 539–576, 2005.

Black, Fischer, and Myron S. Scholes, "The valuation of option contracts and a test of market efficiency," *Journal of Finance* 27(2), 399–418, 1972.

Blazenko, George W., and Andrey D. Pavlov, "Value maximizing hurdle rates for R&D investment," *Economics of Innovation and New Technology,* forthcoming.

Boot, Arnoud W.A., and Anjan V. Thakor, "Banking scope and financial innovation," *Review of Financial Studies* 10(4), pp. 1099–1131, 1997.

Bottazzi, Laura, Marco Da Rin, and Thomas Hellmann, "Who are the active investors? Evidence from venture capital," *Journal of Financial Economics* 89(3), 488–812, 2008.

Caballero, Ricardo, "On the sign of the investment-uncertainty relationship," *American Economic Review* 81(1), 279–288, 1991.

Cameron, Kim S., Jeff DeGraff, Robert E. Quinn, and Anjan V. Thakor, *Competing Values Leadership: Creating Value in Organizations.* Northampton, MA: Edward Elgar, 2006.

Chan, Yuk-Shee, Daniel Siegel, and Anjan V. Thakor, "Learning, Corporate Control and Performance Requirements in Venture Capital Contracts," *International Economic Review* 31(2), 365–381 1990.

Crawford, George, and Bidyut Sen, *Derivatives for Decision Makers: Strategic Management Issues.* New York: John Wiley & Sons, 1996.

157

Dewing, A.S., *Study of Corporate Securities*. New York: Ronald Press, 1934.

Dixit, Avinash K., and Robert S. Pindyck, *Investment under Uncertainty*. Princeton, NJ: Princeton University Press, 1994.

Dodd, David, and Benjamin Graham, *Security Analysis*. New York: McGraw-Hill, 1934.

Elul, Ronel, "Welfare effects of financial innovation in incomplete markets economies with several consumption goods," *Journal of Economic Theory* 65, 43–78, 1995.

Finnerty, John D., "An overview of corporate securities innovation," *Journal of Applied Corporate Finance* 4(4), 23–39, 1992.

Finnerty, John D., "Financial engineering in corporate finance: An overview," *Financial Management* 17, 14–33, 1988.

Finnerty, John D., and Douglas R. Emery, *Debt Management: A Practitioner's Guide*. Cambridge, MA: Harvard University Press, 2001.

Geanuracos, John, and Bill Millar, *The Power of Financial Innovation: Successful Corporate Solutions to Managing Interest Rate, Foreign Exchange Rate and Commodity Exposures on a Worldwide Basis*. New York: Harper Business Press, 1991.

Gompers, Paul A., "Venture capital and private equity," in *Handbook of Corporate Finance: Empirical Corporate Finance* (ed. Espen Eckbo). New York: Elsevier/North-Holland, 2006.

Gompers, Paul A., "Grandstanding in the venture capital industry," *Journal of Financial Economics* 42(1), 133–156, 1996.

Gompers, Paul A., "Optimal investment, monitoring and the staging of venture capital," *Journal of Finance* 50(5), 1461–1489, 1995.

Gompers, Paul, and Josh Lerner, "Venture capital distributions: short-run and long-run reactions," *Journal of Finance* 53(6), 2161–2183, 1998.

Hellmann, Thomas, and Manju Puri, "Venture capital and professionalization of start-up firms: empirical evidence," *Journal of Finance* 15(1), 169–197, 2002.

Hellmann, Thomas, and Manju Puri, "The interaction between product market and financing strategy: The role of venture capital," *Review of Financial Studies* 13(4), 959–984, 2000.

Hellmann, Thomas, and Veikko Thiele, "Incentives and innovation: A multi-tasking approach," University of British Columbia working paper, 2009.

Hendershott, Patric H., and James D. Shilling, "The impact of agencies on conventional fixed-rate mortgage yields," *Journal of Real Estate Finance and Economics* 2(2), 101–115, 1989.

Kane, Edward J., "Technology and the regulation of financial Markets," in *Technology and the Regulation of Financial Markets, Securities, Futures and Banking* (eds. Anthony Saunders and Lawrence J. White), pp. 187–193. Lexington, MA: Lexington Books, 1986,

Kortum, Samuel, and John Lerner, "Assessing the contribution of venture capital to innovation," *Rand Journal of Economics* 31(4), 674–692, 2000.

Lerner, Josh, "Where does State Street lead? A first look at finance patents, 1971–2000," *Journal of Finance* 57(2), 901–903, 2002.

Lerner, Josh, and Peter Tufano, "ALZA and bio-electrical systems (A): Technological and financial innovation," HBS Case No. 293124. Cambridge, MA: Harvard Business Publishing, 1993; see also *http://harvardbusiness.org/product/alza-and-bio-electro-systems-a-technological-and-f/an/293124-PDF-ENG?N∇4294936347&Ntt=financial+strategy*.

Manso, Gustavo, "Motivating innovation," MIT Sloan School of Management working paper, 2008.

Masson, Robert L., and Samuel S. Stratton, *Financial Instruments and Institutions: A Case Book*. New York: McGraw-Hill, 1938.

Matthews, John O., *Struggle and Survival on Wall Street*. New York: Oxford University Press, 1994.

McConnell, John J., and Eduardo S. Schwartz, "The origin of LYONs: A case study in financial innovation," *Journal of Applied Corporate Finance* 4(4), 40–47, 1992.

McDonald, Robert, and Daniel Siegel, "The value of waiting to invest," *Quarterly Journal of Economics* 101(4), 707–728, 1986.

Mehran, Hamid, and Anjan V. Thakor, "Bank capital and value in the cross section," *Review of Financial Studies*, forthcoming.

Merton, Robert C., "On the application of the continuous-time theory of finance to financial intermediation and insurance," *The Geneva Papers on Risk and Insurance* 14(3), 225–261, 1989.

Miller, Merton H., "Financial innovation: The last twenty years and the next," *Journal of Financial and Quantitative Analysis* 21(4), 459–471, 1986.

Molyneux, Philip, and Nidal Shamroukh, *Financial Innovation*. West Sussex, England: John Wiley & Sons, 1999.

Nelson, Richard, "The simple economics of basic scientific research," *Journal of Political Economy* 67(3), 297–306, 1959.

Pindyck, Robert, "Irreversible investment, capacity choice and the value of the firm," *American Economic Review* 78(5), 969–985, 1988.

Rosenberg, Nathan, "Why do firms do basic research (with their own money)?" *Research Policy* 19(2), 165–174, 1990.

Ross, Stephen A., "Institutional markets, financial marketing and financial innovation," *Journal of Finance* 44(3), 541–556, 1989.

State Street Bank v. Signature Financial Group, U.S. Court of Appeals for the Federal Circuit, 47 USPQ2d (BNA) 1596 (Fed. Cir. 1998); see also *http://www.ll.georgetown.edu/federal/judicial/fed/caseBrowse.cfm?caseYear=1998#S.*

Tian, Xuan, and Tracy Y. Wang, "Tolerance for failure and corporate innovation," Indiana University working paper, 2009.

Thakor, Anjan V., "Are financial crises inevitable?" Washington University in St. Louis working paper, 2009.

Tufano, Peter, "Financial innovation: The last 200 years and the next," in *The Handbook of Economics of Finance* (eds. George M. Constantinides, Milton Harris, and René M. Stulz), pp. 307–335. Amsterdam: Elsevier/North-Holland, 2003.

Tufano, Peter, "Financial innovation and first-mover advantages," *Journal of Financial Economics* 25(2), 213–240, 1989.

Additional Readings by Author

Books

Becoming a Better Value Creator: How to Improve Your Company's Bottom Line—and Your Own. Jossey-Bass. First publication date, August 2000.

Competing Values Leadership: Creating Value in Organizations (with Kim S. Cameron, Robert E. Quinn, Jeff Degraff), Edward Elgar Publishing Ltd., 2006.

Creativity at Work (with Jeff DeGraff and Katherine Lawrence). San Francisco: Jossey-Bass. New York: John Wiley & Sons. First publication date, 2002.

A Company of Leaders (with Gretchen M. Spreitzer and Robert E. Quinn). San Francisco: Jossey-Bass. New York: John Wiley & Sons. First publication date, 2002.

Innovation and Growth: What Do We Know? (with Stuart Bunderson, Keith Sawyer, Panos Kouvelis, Betul Lus, Lee Konczak, Signe Spencer, Sam Chun, Nick Argyres, and Anne Marie Knott). Hackensack, NJ: World Scientific. Forthcoming, Fall 2011.

The Value Sphere: The Corporate Executive's Handbook for Creating and Retaining Shareholder Wealth (with John Boquist and Todd Milbourn). Hackensack, NJ: World Scientific. First edition, 2000; Third edition, 2006; Fourth edition, 2009.

Research Papers

"Banking scope and financial innovation" (with Arnoud Boot), *Review of Financial Studies* 10(4), 1099–1131, 1997; to be reprinted as a "CEPR Classic" in forthcoming book (eds: Bruno Biais and Marco Pagano). New York: Oxford University Press.

"Banking structure and financial innovation" (joint with Arnoud Boot), Chapter 14 in *Universal Banking: Financial System Design Reconsidered* (eds., Anthony Saunders and Ingo Walter), pp. 420–430. Irwin Professional Publishing, 1996.

"Creating sustained shareholder value—and dispelling some myths" (with Jeff DeGraff and Robert Quinn), *Financial Times*, Pt. 5, 8(10), 1999.

"EVA and Total Quality Management" (with Jeff Bacidore, John Boquist, and Todd Milbourn), *Journal of Applied Corporate Finance*, 10(2), 81–89, 1997.

"Financial intermediation as a beliefs-bridge between optimists and pessimists" (with Josh Coval), *Journal of Financial Economics* 75(3), 535–570, 2005.

"How do you win the capital allocation game?" (with John Boquist and Todd Milbourn), *Sloan Management Review* 39(2), 59–71, 1998.

"Incentives to innovate and financial crises," forthcoming in *Journal of Financial Economics*.

"Refined economic value added: A better performance measure," *Investor Relations Quarterly* 1(4), 24–29, 1998.

"Security design" (with Arnoud Boot), *Journal of Finance* 48(4), 1349–1378, 1993.

"Shareholder-manager disagreement, animal spirits and corporate investment" (with Toni Whited), *Review of Finance*, 2011.

"The theory of security design" (joint with Arnoud Boot and Todd Milbourn), in *Handbook of Equity Derivatives* (eds., J. C. Francis, W. Toy, and J. G. Whittaker), Irwin Professional Publishing, 1994.

Index

A
ABN AMRO, 101
Abundance approach, 68–69,
    71, 79
Abundance gap, 69
Accountability, 86
Acquisitions. *See* Mergers and
    acquisitions
Acronyms, 59–61, 60t
Advanced Research Projects
    Agency, 127
Advocacy statements, 72
Alignment. *See* Organizational
    alignment
Ambani, Mukesh, 2
Anders, Bill, 143
Anheuser-Busch InBev, 41,
    85–86
Apple, 17–18, 17f
ARAMARK, 108, 108f, 109
Asahi Kasei, 13
Asset turnover, 31–32
Assumptions, 133–135, 136
Autonomy, 86

B
"Bad growth," 6
Bank of America, 95
Barnes & Noble, 135
Bassler, Bonnie, 133
Beijing 2008 Olympics, 117, 118f
Berkshire Hathaway, 17–18, 17f
Bloomberg, Michael, 61, 61f
Blue growth strategies, 96–112
    advantages and disadvantages
        of, 141
    brand development, 106–108

companies with, 42, 95–96
diagram of, 97f
divestitures, 102–106
market niche, 106–108
mergers and acquisitions. *See*
    Mergers and acquisitions
new markets for products and
    services, 108–110
new products and services
    development, 110–112
responding to market changes
    in value driver, 112–113
Brand development, 106–108
Brazil
    educated workforce in, 8
    foreign investment capital
        in, 3
    gross domestic product
        growth rate for, 2
Buffet, Warren, 1, 6, 18
Business paradigm, 133

C
Capital budgeting, 131
Central Nervous for the Earth
    project, 138
China
    educated workforce in, 4, 8
    foreign investment capital
        in, 3
    gross domestic product
        growth rate for, 2
    new products introduced
        into, 109–110
Cisco, 95
Coca-Cola, 17–18, 17f, 18,
    24, 41

Collaborate quadrant, 19–20,
    19f, 33, 76, 150–156t
Commodity businesses, 3, 8
Common language. *See also*
    Language
    complexity affected by, 58–59
    diversity affected by, 61–62
    measurement of things not
        seen or touched through,
        62–64
    power of, 56–64
    sense of community created
        through, 59–61
Communication, 47–49, 71–72,
    72f
Compete quadrant, 20, 22, 32,
    150–156t
Competing Values Framework
    (CVF), 19–24, 150–156t
    Collaborate quadrant of, 19–
        20, 19f, 33, 76, 150–156t
    common language created
        with, 57–58
    company examples of, 35, 35f
    Compete quadrant of, 20, 22,
        32, 150–156t
    Control quadrant of, 19–20,
        19f, 21, 150–156t
    Create quadrant of, 20, 32,
        150–156t
    diagram of, 19f
    innovation rules, 122f, 137f
    interpenetration of
        paradoxes, 142–144, 143f
    investing based on, 30
    leadership style and, 24, 24f
    organizational alignment
        with, 25

Competing Values Framework (*Continued*)
portfolio performance, 36f
profiles, 35f
progression of, 21f
shareholder value and, 30–31
spanning of quadrants in, 26
zones of, 23
Competitive advantage, 44, 87, 120
Constant innovation, 57
Continuing education, 8
Control quadrant, 19–20, 19f, 21, 150–156t
Cooperation, 136
Core competence, 43, 44–45
schematic diagram of, 45f
shared understanding of, 44
Corporate culture, 62–63, 78, 102
Corporate socialism, 89
Coyne, William, 126–127
Create quadrant, 20, 32, 150–156t
Creative work, 126–127
Creativity, 136f
Culture
corporate, 62–63, 78, 102
organizational. *See* Organizational culture
Culture diagnostic instrument, 63
Culture profiles, 63, 63f
CVF. *See* Competing Values Framework

D
Deficit gaps, 69
Dell, 14–15, 15f, 16, 17, 25, 85, 87, 113, 135
Deming, W. Edwards, 127
Developing countries
natural resources of, 4
wealthy individuals in, 2
Dilution of focus, 59
Diverse viewpoints, 124–125, 129
Diversification-causing mergers, 99
Diversity, 61–62

Divestitures, 102–106
Downmarket, 41
Drori, Ze'ev, 134

E
Eberhard, Martin, 134f, 135
Economic profit, 32
Economic value added (EVA), 17–18, 32
Economic value creation, 90
Efficiency
measures of, 31–32
organizational slack effects on, 130
techniques of, 92
Eisner, Michael, 46, 49
"Embracing the enemy," 24
Emerson Electric, 4
Empirical tests
designing of, 31–37
proxies for, 31, 31f
Employees
defiance by, 125–126
development of, 78
execution by, 88–90
firing of, 89
high-performing, 89
hiring of, 88, 129–130
inaction by, 125–126
leadership development of, 78
low-performing, 89
motivation of, 7
performance appraisals for, 88
performance metrics understood by, 91
Enterprise Rent-A-Car, 90–91
Ericsson, 14–15, 15f, 16, 17, 74
European Union (EU), 2
Execution, 83
building blocks of, 83–84
companies that excel in, 85
culture focused on, 86–88, 86f
leadership understanding of, 84–86
people required for, 88–90
steps involved in, 84f
Expertise, 135–136

External alignment of organization, 7, 9, 25
External stakeholders, 20

F
Fat tails, 99
Feedback, 70, 88
Feynman, Richard, 126
Fischer magnetic speed tennis racquet, 123
Focus group, 56–57
Foreign investment capital, 3
Franchising, 13–14
Future growth value, 33

G
Gandhi, Sonia, 61, 61f
Gates, William III, 1, 1f
General Dynamics, 102–106, 143
case study, 103–106
General Electric, 42, 96
General Foods, 45, 106
General Motors, 3
Global positioning satellites, 132, 132f
Global recession, 2
Globalization, 85
Goizueta, Robert, 24
Good growth, 6
difficulties in achieving, 6, 7
stock market rewarding of, 8
Google, 17–18, 17f
Green growth strategies
advantages and disadvantages of, 141
characteristics of, 64
companies with, 42
innovation. *See* Innovation
launching of, 133
net present values, 131
projects involving, 131, 132
risk-taking element of, 133
Gross domestic product (GDP), 2
Gross margin, 31
Group identity, 61
Growth
benefits of, 5
capital market and, 120

good. *See* Good growth
importance of, 145
obstacles to, 9
Growth strategies, 42–43
Blue. *See* Blue growth
strategies
color of, 26f
communication of, 50–51
designing of, 144–145,
144f
examples of, 45–47, 47f
formulation of, 145
Green. *See* Green growth
strategies
implementing of, 144–145,
144f
organizational alignment
and, 49–50, 56
performance metrics linked
to, 90–91
Red. *See* Red growth
strategies
as roadmap, 48
stock price and, 30, 34f
tension caused by, 22
types of, 14
Yellow. *See* Yellow growth
strategies
Growth strategy statement,
47–49
conditions necessary for,
48–49

H

High growth, 7
High-performing organizations,
72
communication in, 73
culture of, 15
positive-to-negative
communication ratio in,
73
Hilzik, Michael, 128
Hiring of employees, 88,
129–130
Hiruta, Shiro, 13
Histogram, 98, 99f
Holtz, Lou, 8
Homo sapiens, 53, 54
Hu Jintao, 61, 61f

Human capital
continuing education of, 8
investments in, 16
Hunt, T. Kendall, 81

I

Ideas
portfolio of, 133
quantity of, 125
Ideo, 124–125, 129–130,
142–143
Imagine Investing phase, of
innovation, 136
Implicit contract, 76
Improve Implementing phase, of
innovation, 137
Inaction by employees, 125–126
Incubate Cooperating phase, of
innovation, 136
India
educated workforce in, 4, 8
foreign investment capital in, 3
GDP, growth rate for, 2
Red growth strategy,
companies in, 82–83
Infosys, 78, 83
Innovation, 32, 120–121
agricultural, 118–119
assumptions broke by,
133–135
combining of features as type
of, 121–124
constant, 57
creative diversity for, 124
CVF, rules of, 122f, 137f
difficulty associated with, 121
diverse viewpoint effects on,
124–125, 129
expertise effects on, 135–136
fragility of, 126–127
future opportunities for,
137–139
in Green growth strategies, 117
importance of, 87
opportunities for, 118–119
organization structure
necessary for, 129
organizational slack, 130,
130f
paradigm, 135

phases of, 136, 137
prepared-core technology, 54
process of, 136–137, 137f
quantity of ideas and, 125
rates of return on, 131–133,
131f
replicability of, 137
reward–punishment system,
125–126
sense of destiny for creative
team involved in, 127–128
SPSS rule of, 128–129, 128f
well-accepted assumptions
broke by, 133–135
Innovative products
common features of, 121
examples of, 121, 123
types of, 122f
Inquiry statements, 72
Internal alignment of
organization, 25
Internal community, 15, 33
Interpenetration of opposites,
142–144, 143f
Invest in Competing phase, of
innovation, 136
Investing, CVF as basis for, 30
Investment banking, 89
Inward focus, 16–17, 20
Ivester, Douglas, 24

J

Jarden Corporation, 29
John Deere, 78, 110–111
Jugaad, 83

K

Kaiser-Hill, 76, 77
Kleiner Perkins Caufield & Byers,
29

L

Language. *See also* Common
language
advantages of, 55
alignment through, 55
invention of, 55
thought process affected by,
55

Leadership
    execution understanding by,
        84–86
    style of, 24, 24f
Leadership development, 64
    employees, 78
    tools for, 77–79
Leapfrog Enterprises, 35, 36
Liquidity Services, 107, 107f, 108
Lotte, in Korea, 109, 109f
Low-performing employees, 89

M

Mahoney, Richard, 13
Management team, 24
Market niche, 106–108
Market shifts, value drivers
        affected by, 112–113
Marks, Michael, 134
McDonald's, 13–14
McKinsey, 14–15, 15f, 16, 17, 74
Mellon, James, 143
Mergers and acquisitions (M&A),
        97–102, 97f
    best practices for, 103f
    corporate culture
        considerations, 102
    growth through, 120
    mature targets, 100
    overpayment of, 101
    risks of, 98, 99–100
    roll-ups, 98
    value creation through, 101
Merton, Robert, 127
Military instability, 3
Mistry, Pranav, 62
Mittal, Lakshmi, 1, 1f, 3
Motivation, employee, 7
Muhleman, Doug, 85–86
Musk, Elon, 134

N

NationsBank, 95
Natural resources, 4
Neanderthals, 53, 54
Negative information, 70
Negative statements, 72
Net assets deployed, 32
Net operating profits after tax,
    32, 33

Net present values, 131
New markets for products and
    services, 108–110
New products and services
    development, 110–112
NOPAT. *See* Net operating profits
    after tax

O

Omega and 2008 Olympics, 42,
    43f
Operating margin, 86–87
Organization(s)
    corporate culture, 62–63, 78
    diversity in, 61–62
    execution by, 85
    growth of, 4
    high-performing. *See* High-
        performing organizations
    internal community of, 15,
        33
    internal processes of, 16
    inward focus by, 16–17, 20
    long-term growth of, 74
    performance-oriented, 89
    priorities of, 58, 59
    Yellow growth strategy
        benefits for, 75–77
Organizational alignment, 7,
    9, 25
    components of, 49
    external, 7, 9, 25
    growth strategy and, 49–50,
        56
    internal, 25
    lack of, 57
    performance metrics and,
        90–91
Organizational change, 68–69
Organizational culture
    execution-focused, 86–88,
        86f
    high-performance, 15
    merger success and,
        correlation between, 102
Organizational performance, 72
Organizational slack, 130, 130f
Organizational tensions
    complex priorities as cause
        of, 58f

growth strategy as cause of,
    22
"Outside the box" thinking, 3

P

Packard, David, 125–126
Paradigm innovation, 135
Performance appraisal, 88
Performance metrics, 150–156t
    employee understanding of,
        91
    growth strategy and, 90–91
    organizational alignment
        and, 90–91
    value creation, 90
Positive factors, 70–73
Positive leadership, 68
Positive statements, 72
Prepared-core technology, 54
Priorities
    considerations for, 84
    doability of, 84
    organizational tensions
        caused by, 58f
    strategic rationale for, 84
Problem-solving approach,
    68–69
Process improvement, 85–86
Proctor & Gamble, 45, 106
Products
    development of, 110–112
    innovative. *See* Innovative
        products
    new markets for, 108–110
Punishments, 86

R

Recession, global, 2
Red growth strategies
    best practices, 92f
    companies with, 42, 81, 82,
        92f
    execution. *See* Execution
    in India, 82–83
    performance metrics. *See*
        Performance metrics
    stability and, 133
Reference point effect, 100
REpower Systems, 82
Resource allocation, 48, 131

Resource commitment, 84
Reward–punishment system, 125–126
Rewards, 86
Risk
    of acquisitions, 98, 99–100
    Green growth strategies and, 133
    high growth and, 7
Rocky Flats Nuclear Arsenal, 76–77
Roll-ups, 98
Ruettgers, Michael, 110

S
Schultz, Howard, 107
Segway, 95–96, 96f
Sense of community, 59–61
Services
    development of, 110–112
    new markets for, 108–110
Shareholders/shareholder value
    CVF and, 30–31
    mergers and acquisitions effect on, 98, 100
Shift tricycle, 123
Silicon Valley, 124–125
Sirius Satellite Radio, 35, 36
SixthSense technology, 62
Sky Windpower, 138
Slack, organizational, 130, 130f
Smith & Wesson Holding Corp., 97
Social networks, 62
Solar panels, 137–138
Southwest, 75–76
S&P 500, 5, 5f
Spanning of quadrants, 26
Stagnation, 5
Starbucks, 14, 45, 46, 106, 107, 113, 135
Stock market, 5, 5f, 8
Stock price, 30

Strategy-Process-Structure Skills (SPSS) rule of innovation, 128–129, 128f
Strategic rationale, 84
Stretch assignments, 78
Sub-Saharan Africa, 2
Sun Pharmaceuticals, 82
Supply water, 119
Sustainable advantage, 83
Suzlon Energy, 82
Swarm engineering, 4
Symbolic thinking, 55

T
Target, 41, 113
Taro Pharmaceutical Industries, 82
Tata Steel, 3, 82, 83
Taylor, Bob, 127, 128
Tempest, Harry, 101
Tesla, 133–134, 134f, 135
Thin Skins, 123
Thompson/Center Arms, 97
3M, 132
Toyota, 87, 113, 120
Tweel, 121, 123

U
US Airways, 75–76

V
Value creation, 31
    mergers and acquisitions, as method of, 101
Value drivers, 42–44
    examples of, 45–47, 47f
    as lead steer business, 43–44
    responding to market changes in, 112–113
    shifts in, 113
    understanding of, 44
    variations in, 47
Value sphere, 45f, 50
Vandebroek, Sophie, 129

Vasco Data Security International, Inc., 81
Volkswagen, 87–88

W
Wal-Mart, 14–15, 15f, 16, 17, 26, 35–36, 41, 42, 113
Walt Disney & Company, 46–47, 49, 50, 67
Welch, Jack, 78
Westinghouse Electric Corporation, 132
W.L. Gore, 124–125, 130
Workforce
    continuing education for, 8
    diversity of viewpoints in, 124, 129
    educated, 4

X
Xerox, 129

Y
Yellow growth strategies
    abundance approach, 68–69, 71, 79
    achieving of, 68–70
    advantages and disadvantages of, 141
    characteristics of, 64
    company examples of, 67, 68, 87–88
    employee investments, 74
    leadership development, 77–79
    long-term growth of organization, 74
    organizational benefits of, 75–77
    principles of, 74
    purpose of, 68

CVF - Competing Values Framework.